THE OPENSPACE AGILITY HANDBOOK

THE USER'S GUIDE

Daniel Mezick

Deborah Pontes

Harold Shinsato

Louise Kold-Taylor

Mark Sheffield

Foreword by Harrison Owen

www.OpenSpaceAgility.com/contact/

OpenSpace Agility™ is a trademark of New Technology Solutions, Inc.

Ordering Information:

Available from Amazon.com and other online stores

Quantity sales: Special discounts are available on quantity purchases by corporations, associations, and others. For details, contact the "Special Sales Department" at the address above.

OpenSpace Agility Handbook / Daniel Mezick, Deborah Pontes, Harold Shinsato, Louise Kold-Taylor, Mark Sheffield. — rev 2.2.1

ISBN 978-0-9848753-3-7 (Paperback)

ISBN 978-0-9848753-4-4 (Kindle)

To every organization inviting transformational change and to the dedicated people whose engagement will make it happen.

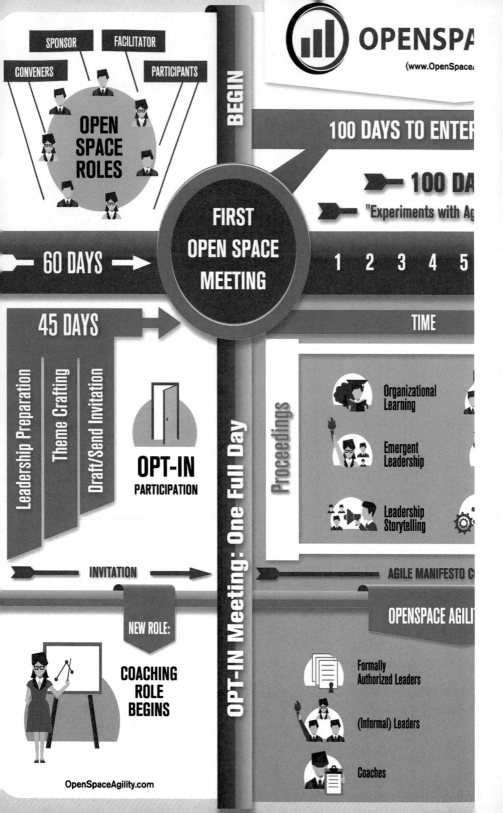

ACE AGILITY™

(eAgility.com)

RPRISE AGILITY

AGILE MANIFESTO

During the 100 days, teams are encouraged to experiment with any and all practices that align with the Agile Manifesto

YS →

"gile practices" →

6 7 8

END

SECOND OPEN SPACE MEETING

30 DAYS →

OpenSpace Agility™ is based on culture-change technology that publishes as open-source and is free to the world.

Learn more at www.Prime-OS.com

Direct Experience

"Experimentation"

Game Mechanics

Theme & Invitation

PROCEEDINGS

- Energy
- Action
- "Escape Velocity"

CONSTRAINTS →

HIGHER PERFORMANCE →

OPT-IN Meeting: Two Full Days

ROLE CHANGE:

COACHING ROLE CHANGES

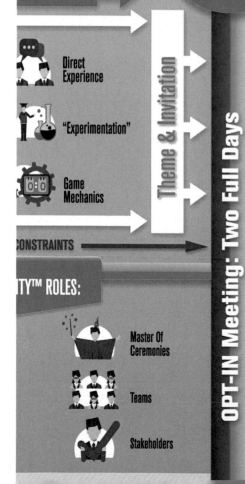

TY™ ROLES:

Master Of Ceremonies

Teams

Stakeholders

Without passion, nobody cares.
Without responsibility, nothing gets done.

–Harrison Owen

Contents

Alphabetical List of Illustrations

Foreword

For those who want their teams and organizations to "be Agile," the approach described in this little book will be helpful.

OpenSpace Agility provides a simple set of steps: Start in open space. Keep that space open for as long as you possibly can. When things close in on you (institutional constraints / claustrophobia), re-open space, as needed, and get the job done. Makes perfect sense to me.

Now, as long as I have known about Agile, Scrum, etc. – it has been clear to me that "being Agile" is simply being fully, consciously, intentionally self organizing. That is total High Performance. And Open Space happens to be (a) fast track to get "there." Not by doing something unique, special, or weird ... but simply by being what we already are. Self organizing.

But it does require a certain letting go of many of the things we thought we should be thinking/doing.

"Thinking of one less thing to do," will give you a good start, and remembering that simplicity is "the art of maximizing the amount of work not done" should carry you along.

Have fun!

Harrison Owen

Camden, Maine

June 2015

Introduction

The Purpose of This Handbook

Welcome to the OpenSpace Agility Handbook. The purpose of this handbook is to serve as a handy reference and pocket guide for those who are adopting Agile or otherwise using OpenSpace Agility to bring strength and vitality to their Agile adoption efforts.

Who This Book Is For

This book is for anyone who is interested in creating more rapid and lasting Agile adoptions. This includes company executives, directors, managers, team members, and the consultants and coaches who serve them.

Preparing To Use This Book

- Have a basic understanding of the Open Space meeting format. Chapter 1 includes a brief user's guide.

- Have a basic understanding of Agile principles and how they can help your organization. The chapter entitled "The Middle (Do)" discusses the Agile Manifesto values and principles.

- Be ready, willing, and able to try OpenSpace Agility to get better results from your Agile adoption.

A bibliography of additional books on topics related to OpenSpace Agility appears at the end of this book.

Visit www.OpenSpaceAgility.com/resources/ for information about OpenSpace Agility training, consulting, and additional resources.

The SPIRIT Book

OpenSpace Agility is inspired by the work of Harrison Owen, specifically by *"SPIRIT: Development and Transformation in Organizations."* It is a great and mighty work, full of keen insights and actionable ideas. It is of strong interest to anyone who is serious about culture architecture and culture design.

The SPIRIT book is available online as a free PDF download at http://www.openspaceworld.com/Spirit.pdf.

Why OpenSpace Agility?

OpenSpace Agility is based on Invitation instead of mandates. Mandates reduce engagement. Invitation and Opt-In Participation increase it. Engagement is essential for a rapid and lasting Agile transformation.

Prescribing practices makes no allowance for what people want, what they think, or what they feel. Prescription reduces engagement. The intelligent and creative people who do the work "check out" and disengage.

Often this pattern is used to implement Agile methods, usually after a small pilot test of Agile with a small team:

- A Formally Authorized Leader says "We are all going Agile. We will be using a specific practice," like Scrum, Kanban, or another practice, method, or framework. The message is that the specified practices must be used by everyone in the organization regardless of whether they are appropriate.

- A Formally Authorized Leader selects a coach based on the coach's expertise with the prescribed practices (typically Scrum). The coach and Agile practices are mandated.

- The people who do the work experience a low sense of control and a low sense of inclusion and belonging. They learn that the new goal is vague, and participation is definitely not opt-in. These experiences trigger people to disengage.

People who create software typically have these characteristics:

- A high level of intelligence

- A tendency to be introverted

- A self-image that includes these stories:

  - "I live to solve problems."

  - "I get paid to solve problems."

  - "I am smart and creative."

  - "I get paid for my technology expertise."

Mandated Agile adoptions tend to repulse the problem-solvers who do the work. These people love to solve problems including process problems like "how to implement Agile at our company." If the organization does not ask what they think, introverts tend not to say.

Often these problem solvers have excellent opinions or ideas. By not asking for their help the organization misses out on their input and creates the potential for considerable resentment. This is a double-barreled negative outcome. The organization loses some of the very best ideas along with a huge opportunity for engagement.

Mandates reduce engagement. Invitation and Opt-In Participation increase it. Engagement is essential for a rapid and lasting Agile transformation.

OpenSpace Agility is based on Invitation instead of mandating specific Agile practices. The OSA pattern calls the Sponsor to:

- Explain the business case for moving in the Agile direction. Explain the challenges the business is facing in terms of competition, pricing pressure, obsolete products, etc.

- Make it clear the enterprise will embrace Agile principles. Explain that specific practices have not been determined.

- Invite everyone involved into the process of writing the Agile transformation story. Communicate clearly that the leaders do not have all the answers and that they are looking for the very best ideas to make the move to Agile genuine, authentic, rapid, and lasting.

- Make it plain that the organization will experiment with various Agile practices. The results of each experiment will be inspected to determine whether to continue the specific practice or framework. If a standard framework like Scrum or Kanban does not meet the needs of the Team or the organization, it can be changed or discarded. The Teams are even free to "roll their own" practices. The only constraint is that the practices must align with the Agile Manifesto.

By implementing Agile principles this way, the people doing the work have a strong sense of control, belonging, and purpose. They engage.

Ongoing Open Space Events

After completing the first OpenSpace Agility cycle the organization will be thinking much more independently and will be much more responsible for its own learning. In symbolic terms, it is important that the Coach depart or take on a different role in the organization. This change in coach status is essential. It is emphasized throughout the passage rite process to show the progress the organization is actually making toward integrating agile ideas into the cultural fabric of the organization.

The last aspect of OSA is the biannual Open Space event. Held in January and July, these events are essential. The whole organization anticipates them. They also serve as cultural initiations for new hires.

By instituting these recurring cultural events on the organization's calendar, the risk of dependency on any one leader is greatly reduced and might even be eliminated. A typical failure pattern in the adoption of Agile occurs when a highly authorized Sponsor and progressive leader exits the company. The 'safe space' necessary to do Agile well departs with him or her.

If the organization continues to hold these recurring Open Space events, the process of Agile transformation can and will continue regardless of who occupies the Formally Authorized Leader roles.

Terminology

These are some of the terms that appear in this book.

Liminality: Being on the threshold of change from one way of thinking and working to a new one. Uncertainty and ambiguity about the new way lead to confusion and stress.

Passage Rite: A ritual for handling the stress of changing to a new way of thinking and working. Passage rites help people enter, understand, and embrace the new way. Open Space meetings and periods of Experiments with Agile practices serve as passage rites.

Communitas: The spirit of community, including feelings of belonging and inclusion.

Master of Ceremonies: The Master of Ceremonies understands the phases of changing from one state to another, reassures the participants of where they are in the transformation, and ensures that they continue to follow the agreed-upon rules of the transformation.

Chapter of Learning: A unit of Organizational Learning with a clear beginning, middle, and end. Chapters of Learning happen between Open Space meetings.

Open Space: A meeting framework that encourages self-organization. Periodic Open Space events are an essential part of OSA.

Open Space Proceedings: Documentation of the sessions contained within an Open Space meeting. Proceedings include words, diagrams, and pictures that describe what was discussed in each session.

Open Space Sponsor: A person in the organization with enough authority to convene and invite people to an Open Space event that lasts at least one full day.

Open Space Facilitator: A person authorized by the Sponsor to assist in executing the meeting. Open Space Facilitators help create an atmosphere of openness and safety and "hold the space" open throughout the entire Open Space meeting.

Coach or Agile Coach: A person hired by the organization to assist in implementing Agile principles, methods, and practices.

Beginning Open Space: An Open Space event that begins a Chapter of Learning. The beginning Open Space is also known as OST-1.

Ending Open Space: An Open Space event that completes and ends a Chapter of Learning. The ending Open Space is also known as OST-2.

Leveling Up: Progressing or graduating to a new level of competence.

Open Space Technology

Open Space Technology is a design for an all-hands meeting. For over 30 years, groups ranging in size from five to 2,000 have opened space and solved complex problems in more than 124 countries around the world.

OST events are most successful when the organization has:

- A puzzle problem of very high importance that is of interest to the group

- A response time of "yesterday"

- The possibility of conflict

This meeting format is perfect for kicking off new Agile adoptions and for re-starting, re-making, and re-booting struggling Agile transformations.

OST is based on Invitation, respect, Opt-In Participation, and above all, self-organization. Honoring these principles leads to high levels of engagement as the Participants join together in writing the story of their Agile transformation. It is their story.

Self organization scales. OST leverages self organization. Frameworks and prescriptions do not scale. Forcing people to do things does not work well.

OpenSpace Agility begins and ends each period of Experimentation in Open Space. These one-day or two-day meetings can consist of 20, 50, or more discussion sessions, depending on the group.

Be Prepared to be Surprised!

A Brief User's Guide to Open Space Technology

Harrison Owen

This excerpt of the BRIEF USER'S GUIDE by Harrison Owen is reprinted here with permission of the author. Serious readers are encouraged to examine the fuller and more complete "OPEN SPACE USER'S GUIDE 3rd EDITION," also from Harrison Owen. It is available in print and Kindle editions.

www.amazon.com/Open-Space-Technology-Users-Guide/dp/1576754766

The Requirements of Open Space

Open Space Technology requires very few advance elements. There must be a clear and compelling theme, an interested and committed group, time and a place, and a leader. Detailed advance agendas, plans, and materials are not only un-needed, they are usually counterproductive. This brief User's Guide has proven effective in getting most new leaders and groups off and running. While there are many additional things that can be learned about operating in Open Space, this will get you started. Some material has been included here which also appears in the book in order to present a relatively complete picture.

THE THEME – Creation of a powerful theme statement is critical, for it will be the central mechanism for focusing discussion and inspiring participation. The theme statement, however, cannot be a lengthy, dry, recitation of goals and objectives. It must have the capacity to inspire participation by being specific enough to indicate the direction, while possessing sufficient openness to allow for the imagination of the group to take over.

There is no pat formulation for doing this, for what inspires one group will totally turn off another. One way of thinking about the theme statement is as the opening paragraph of a truly exciting story. The reader should have enough detail to know where the tale is headed and what some of the possible adventures are likely to be. But "telling all" in the beginning will make it quite unlikely that the reader will proceed. After all, who would read a story they already know?

THE GROUP – The group must be interested and committed. Failing that, Open Space Technology will not work. The key ingredients for deep creative learning are real freedom and real responsibility. Freedom allows for exploration and experimentation, while responsibility ensures that both will be pursued with rigor. Interest and commitment are the prerequisites for the responsible use of freedom. There is no way that we know of to force people to be interested and committed. That must be a precondition.

One way of ensuring both commitment and interest is to make participation in the Open Space event completely voluntary. The people who come should be there because they want to be there. It is also imperative that all participants know what they are getting into before they arrive. Obviously they can't know the details of discussions that have yet to take place. But they can and should be made aware of the general outlines. Open Space is not for everybody, and involuntary, non-informed participation is not only a contradiction in terms, it can become very destructive.

This raises the obvious question of what to do with those people whom you want to involve, but who, for whatever reason, do not share your desire. There are two possibilities. The first is to schedule two sessions, and trust that the first one will be so rewarding that positive word of mouth testimony will draw in the recalcitrant. The alternative is to respect the wishes of those involved. In the final analysis it remains true that genuine learning only takes place on the basis of interest and commitment, and there is absolutely no way to force any of that.

The size of the group is not absolutely critical. However, there does seem to be a lower limit of about 20. Less than 20 participants, and you tend to lose the necessary diversity which brings genuine interchange. At the upward end of the scale, groups of 400 work very well, and there is no reason to believe that number could not be increased.

SPACE – The space required is critical, but need not be elaborate or elegant. Comfort is more important. You will need a room large enough to hold the entire group, with space to spare in which the participants may easily move about. Tables or desks are not only unnecessary, but will probably get in the way. Movable chairs, on the other hand, are essential.

The initial setup is a circle with a large, blank wall somewhere in the room. The wall must be free from windows, doors, drapes, and with a surface that permits taping paper with masking tape. The wall should also be long enough so that the total group may stand before it, and never be more than three to four deep. The center of the circle is empty, for after all we are talking about Open Space.

If the room is very large, additional break-out areas may not be required, but they are always helpful. Best of all is the sort of environment in which there is an abundance of common space. If you are going to use a conference center or hotel, find one with plenty of conversation nooks, lobbies, and open grounds, where people may meet and work undisturbed, and without disturbing others.

TIME – The time required depends on the specificity of result you require. Even a large group can achieve high levels of interaction combined with a real sense of having explored the issues in a matter of eight hours. However, if you want to go deeper than that, reaching firm conclusions and recommendations (as would be the case for strategic planning or product design), the time required may stretch to two or three days.

More important than the length of time is the integrity of the time. Open Space Technology will not work if it is interrupted. This means that "drop-ins" should be discouraged. Those who come must be there at the beginning, and stay for the duration if at all possible. By the same token, once the process begins, it cannot be interrupted by other events or presentations. These might come before or afterwards, but never in the middle.

The Basic Structure

Although it is true that an Open Space event has no pre-determined agenda, it must have an overall structure or framework. This framework is not intended to tell people what to do and when. Rather, it creates a supportive environment in which the participants can solve those issues for themselves. Minimal elements of this framework include: Opening, Agenda Setting, Open Space, and Conclusion. These elements will suffice for events lasting up to a day. Longer events will require the addition of Morning Announcements, Evening News, and probably a Celebration.

A standard Open Space Design using all these elements appears below. If the event you anticipate lasts longer than the time indicated, simply replicate the middle day. If shorter, you will find that an Opening, Open Space, and Conclusion will suffice. Generally speaking, the minimum time required is five hours, but that is cutting it rather close.

OPENING – We have found that a very informal opening works well, especially if the group involved is an intact work group. An evening meal and a time for catch-up conversation will effectively set the stage. Should the group not have any prior association, the simple device of having all the participants introduce themselves by giving their names and telling a short story from their lives to illustrate who they are will usually do the job. Detailed and involved "icebreaking" exercises do not seem to work very well, and more to the point, set the wrong tone. After all, we want Open Space.

AGENDA SETTING – This is the time for the group to figure out what it wants to do. The details for this procedure are given below.

OPEN SPACE – is exactly what the words imply, open space and time for the group to do its business. There is literally nothing here at the start.

ANNOUNCEMENTS – A short period every morning for the group to catch up on what it is doing, where, when, and how. Nothing elaborate, no speeches, just the facts, nothing but the facts.

EVENING NEWS – This is usually a time for reflection and occasionally fun. Not to be confused with a formal report-out session, the approach is "What's the story?" — with participants voluntarily providing the tale.

CELEBRATION – If your Open Space event is like all the ones we have seen, particularly multi-day affairs, by the last night it will be time to celebrate, otherwise known as having a party. Even in "serious" undertakings like preparation of the corporate strategic plan, when it is over, it is over, and people will enjoy celebrating that fact. We suggest doing the celebration in the spirit and manner of the rest of the event. All of which means don't plan it in advance. It may be worthwhile to have some taped music if your people are inclined to dance, but other than that you will undoubtedly find that the talent you need is already available in the folks you have. Use it. Skits, songs, and humorous reviews of what has happened will amply the evening and add to the learning experience.

CLOSING – We try to keep the closing simple and serious. Simple in that there are no formal presentations and speeches. But serious, for this is the time for announcing commitments, next steps, and observations about what the event has meant. The closing event is best conducted in a circle with no "head table." Start anywhere, and go around the circle allowing each participant, who wants to, the opportunity to say what was of significance and what they propose to do. But do make it clear that nobody has to say anything. In very large groups, hearing from everybody is obviously impossible, but two or three folks may be asked to volunteer.

FORMAL REPORTS – The formal report-out session has apparently become a fixture of conference life. However, we find it to be boring and generally non-productive. There is never enough time for each group to say all they wanted to, and if sufficient time is allocated, the majority of conference participants are uninterested at any given time. As an alternative, we recommend using a simple word processing system, a computer conferencing system, or both.

In a recent conference 200 participants created 65 task force reports (a total of 200 pages) which were available as the participants left the conference. Mechanically, all that is required is a bank of computers (low-powered laptops will do) and a request to each group organizer to enter the results of their deliberations into the system. They can either type it in themselves, or for the "nontypables," a small group of secretaries will do the job. We print out each report as it is entered and hang it on the wall, providing an ongoing, real-time record of the discussions. The obvious advantage here is that participants find out what is happening, as it is happening, rather than waiting until the end when it is too late. Of course, having the proceedings at the end of conference, rather than six months later, is a pleasant and positive surprise.

MEALS – You will notice that meals are not listed on the agenda, nor are there any coffee breaks. The reason is quite simple: once the conference starts to operate in small groups, there is usually never a time when something of substance is not going on. And in accord with the Third Principle, it will take place in its own time. All of this creates a small, but not insoluble, problem for such things as meals and coffee-breaks. Our solution has been to have coffee and other refreshments available in the main meeting room, so people partake when they are ready. No need for the whole group to get into lockstep, and stop an important discussion just because it is coffee-break time. Likewise with meals. We suggest buffets, open and available over a several hour period, so people can eat when they want to. There are two exceptions to the flexible meal/coffee-break schedule: an opening dinner if there is one, and dinner on the last night.

The whole point is that the pacing and timing of the conference must be determined by the needs of the group and its learning process, and not by the requirements of the kitchen.

————

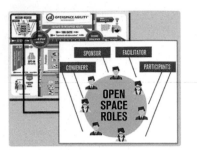

Open Space Roles

Open Space Technology provides a lightweight template for arranging and holding great gatherings and meetings.

OST only has four roles. These roles define boundaries and provide guidance about opening up space for self-organization to occur. There is no coercion in Open Space.

The **Sponsor** authorizes the event, makes it clear that the organization values the event and its outcomes, and grants authority and responsibility to the Facilitator for presiding over the event. Then the Sponsor gets out of the way and lets the Open Space event unfold.

The **Facilitator** receives authority from the Sponsor to execute the event from start to finish. The Facilitator retains authority and responsibility for holding the space and keeping it open for self-organization. All of the remaining authority and responsibility for the success of the event are transferred to the Participants.

Participants self-organize as they decide to attend sessions, participate in discussions, and share the outcomes with the rest of the organization.

Conveners are Participants who propose and initiate session topics for small-group discussions. Within each session the Convener is responsible for keeping the session open for input from all Participants. Conveners are also responsible for collecting Proceedings.

Authority and Self-Organization in Open Space

Every social situation has an "authority dimension." Open Space creates a very social situation, and therefore Open Space has this "authority dimension."

The dynamics and distribution of authority in Open Space are really very simple. There are three basic roles: the Sponsor, the Facilitator, and the Participants.

- The Sponsor (aka Host) welcomes the group of Participants and authorizes the event.

- The Sponsor then hands over authority to run the meeting to the Facilitator.

- The Facilitator, in turn, then directly hands that authority over to the Participants: to each individual in the group. The Participants play a very active role in the "management" of the event.

The Facilitator does hold back one small piece of the authorization that comes from the Sponsor.

That one piece of authority held by the Facilitator is the authority to "hold the space." To "hold the space" is to "hold the space open" or to "maintain openness."

How this "holding the space" is actually achieved can take many forms, and it varies from Facilitator to Facilitator. It also varies from situation to situation. What we know for sure is that, in an Open Space event, at least in theory, Participants are free to enjoy the event as they see fit. Participants engage in the event as they wish, without interference from others who might tell them what they "should" do.

Open Space events encourage very high levels of self-organization by creating a set of rich and fertile conditions where self-organization can emerge spontaneously.

Sponsor

An effective Sponsor must be:

- A Formally Authorized Leader with enough authority to schedule an all-day meeting

- Willing to fill the Sponsor role completely by taking up all of the duties and tasks that come with it

- Passionately ready to process and act on the Proceedings with others immediately after the event

The Sponsor has important responsibilities before, during, and after the Open Space event.

Before

- Invite others to help craft the Theme and discover who feels passionate and responsible about the design and planning of the Open Space event.

- Draft and send the Invitation to all employees who will be affected by the Agile transformation. By personally sending the Invitations the Sponsor indicates the importance of the event. Delegating this responsibility would indicate that the Sponsor has "more important things to do."

- Engage in Leadership Storytelling about the Open Space event, its purpose, and actions that are taken based on its outcomes.

During

- Welcome all Participants and thank them for accepting the Invitation to be actively involved in the Agile transformation.

- Communicate the opportunities and threats that the organization faces.

- Signal that the work of the meeting is extremely important. Words, facial expressions, body posture, tone of voice, and authenticity are important signals. People throughout the organization are watching for these signals. They indicate how the Sponsor really feels about the event and the Agile transformation.

- Introduce the Facilitator, hand off administration of the Open Space, and get out of the way.

- Participate in the Open Space as a peer without coercing the other Participants.

After

- Put the Proceedings into everyone's hands as soon as possible, typically by sending an email message with a link to the document. Distributing the complete Proceedings quickly indicates that the Sponsor values the Open Space outcomes and the Agile transformation.

- Call the steering team together to examine and immediately act upon the Proceedings.

- Engage in Leadership Storytelling that supports the organization's goals for Agile transformation.

It is essential that the Sponsor and other Formally Authorized Leaders continuously signal strong support for the entire process.

The best way to demonstrate executive support is to consider and act without delay on the issues identified in the Proceedings.

Facilitator

According to Harrison Owen, "The key ingredients for deep creative learning are real freedom and real responsibility." Open Space Technology creates a safe and open forum where Participants are free to identify, discuss, and solve issues that matter most to them. Participants are responsible for making the event successful. The Facilitator's job is to serve the Participants by maintaining or "holding" the space.

The Facilitator is formally authorized by the Sponsor to facilitate and administer the event. Ideally the Facilitator should have no other authority whatsoever within the organization. In turn the Facilitator formally authorizes the Participants to identify, discuss, and solve issues related to the Theme.

The Facilitator prepares the room in advance so that the Participants will have the environment and support they need for creative learning:

- Chairs in a circle facing the middle of the room, which is empty except for some blank pieces of paper and markers.

- A large empty wall where session descriptions may be taped or pinned. The agenda will take shape here.

- Posters around the room displaying the Theme, the Four Principles, the One Law, and reminders to "Be Prepared to be Surprised."

After receiving formal authorization from the Sponsor, the Facilitator welcomes the Participants, briefly describes Open Space, and then holds the space.

The Facilitator provides basic guidance about Open Space:

- Any Participant may become a Convener by proposing and scheduling a discussion about a topic they are passionate about. Conveners are encouraged to document the discussions so that the discussions and recommendations can be shared with the rest of the organization.

- Participants will be invited to select and attend the sessions that interest them.

- The Four Principles and the One Law.

- "We'll see you all back here for the closing session."

Then the Facilitator gets out of the way, expecting, allowing, and trusting the Participants to self-organize.

During the rest of the event, the Facilitator does whatever is beneficial to maintain the atmosphere of Open Space. This may mean walking around to see what is happening. It may also mean picking up trash and otherwise removing distractions that might interfere with the atmosphere.

At the end of the event, the Facilitator creates the conditions for the Closing Circle and invites Participants to share what they learned and what actions they plan to take.

Participants

Participants decide whether to attend the Open Space event, its sessions, and other conversations.

The Open Space Facilitator formally authorizes each Participant to decide how to participate. In return, each Participant agrees to be responsible for the success of the event. Participants self-organize to explore aspects of the Theme that they are most passionate about and to share the results of those discussions with the rest of the organization.

Participation in Open Space events is completely voluntary. The people who opt in to attend are there because they want to be. This is true regardless of whether they support, tolerate, or resist Agile adoption. Open Space gives Participants the freedom to identify, discuss, and solve the issues that matter most to them.

Each Participant is free to choose which sessions and other conversations to join.

Participants are authorized to become Conveners and propose session topics.

Conveners

Conveners are Participants who initiate small-group sessions and/ or informal discussions. They emerge as (Informal) Leaders. Each Participant is free to become a Convener by:

- Proposing a topic and adding it to the Marketplace

- Negotiating with other Conveners as necessary to determine where and when the discussion will take place

- Opening the discussion, welcoming the Participants, and inviting them to contribute to the discussion

- Ensuring that the results of the discussion are captured and recorded so they can become part of the Proceedings

Convening a discussion means explaining the topic and keeping the session open for free and open dialogue. It does not mean assembling an audience to hear what the Convener wants to say.

Additional guidelines for each Convener to keep in mind:

- It's OK to discuss a topic in more than one session.

- If no Participants choose to attend your session, you may decide to participate in another session or use the time for personal reflection about the topic – your solutions may end up becoming top priorities.

- It's OK if Participants leave or join during the session – they're just following the Law of Two Feet.

The Four Principles

Whoever comes is the right people.

Whatever happens is the only thing that could have.

Whenever it starts is the right time.

When it's over, it's over.

(Plus One)

Wherever it happens is the right place.

The One Law

If, during our time together, you find yourself in any situation where you are neither learning nor contributing, use your two feet and go to some more productive place.

Be Prepared to be Surprised!

Chapter 2

OpenSpace Agility

OpenSpace Agility is a repeatable technique for rapid and lasting Agile transformation. It works with what you and your organization are currently doing and can be added at any time.

OSA incorporates the power of Invitation, Open Space, Game Mechanics, passage rites, storytelling, and more so your Agile adoption can actually take root. OSA is based on people, then practices. You can use any Agile practices or frameworks with it.

Rapid, effective, and lasting Agile adoptions are powered by human engagement, not by frameworks, consultants, or coaches.

You can start using OSA today to improve your current Agile adoption, or to get it right the first time.

Is your Agile adoption in trouble? OSA can help.

Just getting started with Agile? OSA is the way to begin.

OSA is not complicated.

It starts and ends in Open Space.

It ENGAGES people.

Start and end in an all-hands Open Space meeting of at least one day. In between, implement Agile in an Agile way. Do experiments with practices that align with and are confirmed by the Agile Manifesto.

This method is iterative and incremental, just like Agile itself. There is a clear beginning, middle, and end to each step in the transformation.

Preparation

- Assess the organization's alignment and willingness to experiment with Agile and Open Space.

- Coach the Sponsor in what to say and do.

- Make sure the Sponsor commits to take immediate action on the Proceedings and speaks that commitment to the organization.

- Ensure that the Sponsor and other leaders generate and tell stories that support the overall Agile effort.

Begin in Open Space

- Formally Authorized Leaders plan for OpenSpace Agility. They determine the Theme, define an Experimentation period of 60-100 days, and authorize the organization to experiment with various Agile practices. The leaders invite everyone in the organization to participate. The intent is to allow everyone to engage.

- The first event is an all-hands Open Space meeting. Attendance is 100% voluntary. Everyone at all authorization levels in each affected business unit is invited to attend. As a result there is a huge mixing of people and ideas.

- In the closing circle at the end of OST-1 everyone learns that OST-2 will happen in about 100 days. Everyone learns that the organization is serious about inspecting results and making adjustments.

Experiment and Learn

- Invite Teams to suspend disbelief, act as if, and pretend that Agile principles and practices can work.

- Teams understand what they are authorized to do. Then they commit to experimenting with Agile practices.

- Encourage Experimentation.

- Formally Authorized Leaders engage in deliberate Leadership Storytelling that supports the Experimentation.

- The Teams experiment with using any practices that align with the Agile Manifesto: the four values and twelve principles. This is the single firm constraint. There are no others. If an experimental practice obviously offends the spirit of the Manifesto, it is out of bounds. If a practice does not align with the Manifesto, it is not a valid practice for Experimentation during this period.

- Other than the single constraint and the "100 days," there is no prescription of practices. Teams find practices that work within the boundary of the Manifesto.

- Emphasize learning reinforced by Formally Authorized Leaders, learning what Agile practices are and how to use them in ways that fit the organization's mission, current position, and context.

- Ideally, the Formally Authorized Leadership team also Experiments with Agile practices like short daily meetings, Iterations, and retrospectives. This sends all the right signals and tells a coherent leadership story.

End in Open Space

- After the "100 days" of Experimentation and learning there is another Open Space. This all-hands, 100% opt-in meeting is a rite of passage, a look back and a look ahead. One chapter ends and a new one begins.

- The previous chapter is closed, and a new chapter of Experimentation opens. By OST-2, Teams have unanimous agreement on what is working well and how they want to work. And they start noticing what must change.

- A massive amount of self-organization occurs. The entire organization begins to shift away from mediocrity and toward excellence via continuous improvement.

- The result is huge progress across the entire (invited) group.

- Each Open Space event closes one chapter of learning and opens another. This cycle repeats periodically as the organization inspects and adapts.

After completing the first OpenSpace Agility cycle the organization will be thinking much more independently and will be much more responsible for its own learning.

Plan the Next Cycle

The last aspect of OSA is the biannual Open Space event. Held in January and July, these events are essential. The whole organization anticipates them. They also serve as a cultural initiation for new hires.

Summary

- OpenSpace Agility is really very simple. It scales. It's not complicated. Each cycle begins and ends in Open Space. In between, learning is generated and informs the next cycle of improvement.

- OSA promotes self-management and self-organization.

- Scale is achieved by the organization itself, by the workforce you already have. Your people become highly engaged and do everything that needs to be done.

- Dependency on expensive and highly paid consultants (who typically have little or no real stake in your future) is greatly reduced.

OSA works for one simple reason: it generates extremely high levels of engagement across your entire organization. This engagement is essential to the success of your program. No other method generates more engagement than OSA does.

OpenSpace Agility is designed to:

- Create a rapid, effective, and lasting Agile transformation.

- Encourage the entire organization to reach a state of self-sustaining, freestanding Agility.

- Save money by reducing the number of coaches (and coaching days) needed to get solid results – and continuous improvement.

OpenSpace Agility works with what you are doing now and can be added at any time.

———

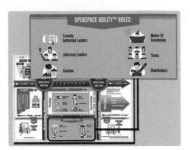

OpenSpace Agility Roles

OpenSpace Agility is a lightweight pattern for empowering and guiding authentic Agile transformation.

OSA has five roles. These roles define boundaries, provide guidance about who is authorized to do what, and open up space for self-organization to occur. There is no coercion in OSA.

The **Master of Ceremonies** provides reassurance and guidance about "where we are now." This role does not hold any authority within the organization.

Coaches model how good facilitation should look. They are available to provide guidance as it is requested. They are not authorized to force or inflict help.

Stakeholders are affected by the adoption of Agile principles and practices. They also benefit from the products that are being developed.

Formally Authorized Leaders receive their leadership authority explicitly from the organization. They may assign formal authority to people who report to them directly or indirectly.

(Informal) Leaders receive their authorization informally from the group. These leaders emerge as members of the group invite them to be responsible for what they care about, and they do so.

Teams include the developers, product owners, and everyone else who is experimenting with Agile practices.

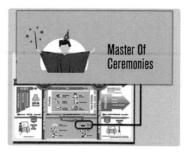

Master of Ceremonies

The Master of Ceremonies presides over the passage-rite event, providing guidance about "where we are now." Passage rites are cultural ceremonies that take individuals and groups from one "steady state" to another. In between, there is a transition and transformation.

OpenSpace Agility borrows from the social sciences in general and cultural anthropology in particular. OSA implements rites of passage. The organization starts the experience one way, experiences a change in status, and exits the experience as something new and different.

Passage rites evoke feelings of communitas, the spirit of community. Everyone agrees to the rules of the game, and then the entire group goes through the experience together. This shared experience tends to elevate feelings of membership, belonging, and communitas.

Transitions are often very triggering for participants. No longer "here," and not yet "there," people in a state of ambiguous transition can often feel very lost.

The Master of Ceremonies provides reassurance and guidance through these difficult transitions. The Master of Ceremonies should behave in such a way as to be perceived as a wise guide and encourager, not as being in charge or being an enforcer.

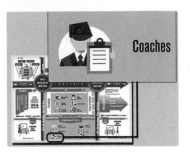

Coaches

Coaches model good facilitation.

OpenSpace Agility Coaches invite others to learn these skills.

Each OSA Coach is typically responsible for coaching specific Teams, usually not more than three at a time. During the "100 Days" of Experiments with Agile practices, the Coaches provide facilitation and guidance and may administer various kinds of before-and-after assessments. These assessments serve as diagnostics and metrics.

Several materials at www.OpenSpaceAgility.com/resources can help the Coach figure out where Teams (and the organization) are and where they can go next in a reasonable amount of time.

The coaching role is about assisting others in learning the Agile principles and helping with the execution of experiments with specific practices.

When beginning with an organization that is mostly new to Agile, starting with strong momentum is important. This means being present almost every day. As soon as possible, the Coach should be absent at least some of the time. For example, after successfully training some employees to be Facilitators (or Scrum Masters if they are doing Scrum), it is a very good idea for them to experience life without the Coach for a day or two. This helps prepare the Team for when the Coach leaves at the end of the "100 days."

Concerning Executives

Coaches work closely with Teams and must also coach the Formally Authorized Leaders in how to think, and especially how to behave.

Each OSA Coach must pay careful attention to the levels of support across the entire executive team. Strong support from the CEO or other top executive does not mean that everyone on the leadership team agrees. Resistant executives can and will work to slow down progress. Agile changes the game for everyone in the organization. Not all players will be entirely comfortable with the changes.

The executive team, including the Agile supporters and resisters, may benefit from coaching about demonstrating:

- "We executives are learning Agile principles and experimenting with Agile practices."

- "We need your skills, passions, abilities, and energy to make Agile successful."

- "You are encouraged and free to make suggestions at any level without negative consequences. We will act upon the most important concerns reflected in the Open Space Proceedings."

- "We are responsible for high-level organizational direction, decisions, and results. You will have free rein to implement some things. You will need to get approval for some things. Some suggestions may not be able to be implemented at this time."

- "We are prepared to be surprised. Amaze us!"

OSA Coaches do not "inflict help" on Teams, managers, or executives. They work closely with those who signal strong interest in learning Agile principles and practices.

Stakeholders

A Stakeholder is anyone in the organization who is affected by the introduction of Agile principles and practices.

Genuine Agile principles and supporting practices will eventually impact the organizational culture in every dimension.

Everyone in the organization is a Stakeholder.

It is critically important to invite everyone to the beginning and ending Open Space events. OpenSpace Agility makes sure that all affected parties may participate. The organization cannot successfully force Agile or any other transformation. What it can do is create fertile conditions for engagement and growth.

The best way to include Stakeholders is to invite them to participate in the Open Space events. What they do next is up to them.

Stakeholders can provide rich feedback. Without their involvement, the organization will miss significant opportunities for improvement.

Stakeholder feedback and engagement are essential. Genuine, authentic Invitation is the best way to get it.

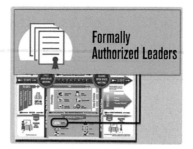

Formally Authorized Leaders

Organizational charts, job titles, and job descriptions formally define roles, authority, and responsibilities for each person in the organization. Formally Authorized Leaders have permission to make decisions directing people, policies, and dollars.

OpenSpace Agility depends on a formally authorized Sponsor with substantial authority within the organization. This leader must be able to ensure that the first and second Open Space events and all experiments are clearly optional with no formal consequences for opting out. The Sponsor must signal very clearly that OSA is based on Invitation and Opt-In Participation.

High-ranking formal leaders are tasked by the Sponsor to act on the top ideas in the Proceedings of OST-1 and OST-2. As the Sponsor and Formal Leaders encourage and nurture engagement in Open Space, (Informal) Leaders emerge and increase the pace of the Agile initiative and experiments toward high performance.

People watch leaders, especially Formally Authorized Leaders. Everyone in the organization will be watching the behavior of these leaders. By making their behavior coherent with the organization's intention to achieve high performance and agility, these Formally Authorized Leaders are actively helping write the story of the organization's success.

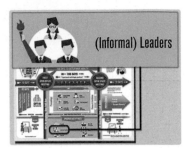

(Informal) Leaders

Positions of leadership include authority and responsibility to act. Formally Authorized Leaders are empowered by their positions to make decisions and take actions directing people, policies, and dollars. Other leaders emerge based on their relationships and interactions with people in the organization.

Informal authority is assigned, projected, demanded, declined, and withdrawn consciously and unconsciously as people work together. When it feels safe, people accept and embrace the opportunity to become or follow (Informal) Leaders.

These leaders are the life and blood of OpenSpace Agility. They bring the best ideas directly from the actual contexts where work is being done. Those ideas are based on their abilities and passion and may not have been seen before.

It can be challenging to allow people to take on this critical role. Speeches and policies about employees empowerment seldom do enough to overcome old habits of waiting for permission.

Open Space Technology and OSA use Game Mechanics that make it safe for individuals to experiment with leading. During each Open Space event, everyone in the organization gets to experiment with leading and following emergent leaders in the specific contexts they care about. This breaks the bottleneck of every initiative needing to pass through the formal leadership. It dramatically increases engagement and leads to Higher Performance.

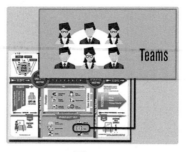

Teams

Software development Teams are the initial focus of most Agile adoptions. In OpenSpace Agility, Teams experiment with Agile practices for about 100 days as they tune and adjust their behavior in the direction of continuous improvement.

Teams might be large or small. They may or may not decide to use Scrum or Kanban. During the period of Experimentation, the primary thing that is generated is learning. All too often there is pressure to get a software or product delivery out the door, even as the Teams are figuring out new ways to do so. Yes, Teams are expected to continue to deliver as they are learning. In OSA the Teams intentionally choose to try specific practices during the period of Experimentation.

You might wonder: "How can all these Teams stay in sync if they are each allowed to do something different?"

The answer is surprisingly simple: by periodically inviting ALL the Teams and ALL the Stakeholders into Open Space. There is no need for central control. When people show up passionate, responsible, and fully engaged, the best ideas get heard and the best courses of action are identified and acted upon.

By the time OST-2 rolls around, the Teams are very aware of what needs to be done for everyone to remain in sync.

CHAPTER 3

The Beginning (Plan)

Concepts

- Using Invitations to increase engagement

- Preparing for the first Open Space

- Game Mechanics

Context

- The Sponsor and other highly authorized leaders are confident that Agile and Open Space can help the organization solve critical challenges.

- Agile is a different way of thinking about getting work done. Some people in the organization fear or resist changing.

- Open Space allows people to change without being forced to change. This is very different than issuing mandates.

- The Sponsor and other leaders must clearly demonstrate support for experimenting with Agile, and must clearly authorize the organization to participate.

Tasks

- Craft the Theme for OST-1

- Draft and send the OST-1 Invitation

- Hold OST-1 and act on the Proceedings

Invitation

OpenSpace Agility is built upon the power of Invitation.

Invitation must be authentic. There must be no negative consequences for declining.

The Invitation must state clear goals, rules, and feedback so that each recipient can make an informed decision about whether to join.

Issuing an authentic Invitation instead of a mandate demonstrates respect for the other person. Respect for people is a core, bedrock value of Lean and Agile principles.

Issuing an Invitation is transferring a small amount of decision-making authority to the individual. When this is done authentically with no repercussions for opting out, it demonstrates that everyone has an important part in writing the story of the organization's progress.

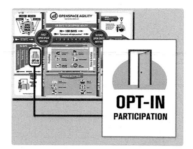

Opt-In Participation

As Harrison Owen says: "Without passion, nobody cares. Without responsibility, nothing gets done."

Passionate and responsible people who choose to participate can and will show up to do the hard work of leading the Agile transformation. Allow those people to opt-in by issuing authentic Invitations instead of mandates.

Being invited lets the person control what happens next. It authorizes the person to decide whether to join the group of people who are writing the story of the organization's progress.

Feeling a sense of control and a sense of belonging lead to becoming and remaining engaged. The power of Opt-In Participation, choosing to accept a genuine Invitation, cannot be underestimated.

Employees who choose to opt in have a high degree of ownership in the outcome. They have an opportunity to demonstrate their passion and take responsibility for getting things done.

This naturally increases engagement across the organization.

One of the best outcomes of Opt-In Participation is data about whether the organization is ready and willing to move in the stated direction.

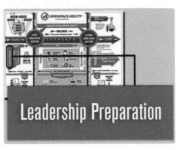

Leadership Preparation

The Sponsor, executives, and other high-ranking leaders must prepare for what will happen during the Open Space events and the Agile transformation. Otherwise the implementation will fail.

These leaders must communicate extremely well to the entire enterprise before, during, and after the Open Space events of any OpenSpace Agility implementation.

Leadership Preparation is an incremental process. Steps include:

- Understanding and accepting the differences between a mandate and an Invitation and the huge differences in the typical results of each style.

- Embracing the Open Space meeting format and their role as Sponsor (host) of these events.

- Engaging in Leadership Storytelling before, during, and after Open Space events.

- Supporting and encouraging (Informal) Leaders and allowing them to emerge.

OSA contains a set of guidelines, resources, and artifacts that support the ongoing work of educating the leaders as they engage and help write the organization's Agile transformation story.

The leaders will also experience liminality and communitas. They will need a Coach. They will also benefit from encouragement and reassurance from the Master of Ceremonies.

Coaching Role Begins

OpenSpace Agility is designed to help organizations learn how to embrace Agile principles as they experiment with Agile practices. An essential part of this design is the Coach (or coaching team), who must:

- Teach Agile values and principles and how to apply them.

- Deliver guidance on specific practices (for example, Scrum, Kanban) and why these practices might be useful for a given Team or context.

- Deliver specific services to executives and Teams, such as meeting facilitation and learning exercises.

- Model good patterns including respect, adherence to Agile principles, storytelling, and Game Mechanics.

- Identify who is willing to learn new skills. Invite them to enter into a mentored relationship including learning by watching, doing, and private conversations with the Coach on a day-by-day basis.

The Coaching role begins with Leadership Preparation before the first Open Space event. It continues through "100 days" of Experimentation and OST-2. Then the Coaching role ends as the Teams take responsibility for implementing what they have learned. At that time the Coach could begin working with a different set of Teams or leave the organization. A new group of Coaches can then fill the coaching role for the next period of learning.

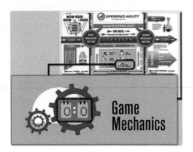

Game Mechanics

The best games have clear goals, rules, a visible scoreboard, and Opt-In Participation. The players know why they are there, what needs to be done, and how well they are doing. The fans join in and tell stories about "our" successes and about where "we" need to improve.

Jane McGonigal described Game Mechanics in *"Reality Is Broken."* These principles also apply to meetings, tasks, projects, and initiatives. Every strong game has:

- **Purpose**: Clear goals explain the purpose of the game. In OpenSpace Agility the purpose is continuous improvement and Organizational Learning by experimenting with Agile practices. Clear goals answer the "why" questions. "Why are we attending this meeting?" "Why are we doing this?" "Why are we doing it this way?"

- **Rules**: Explicit rules tell participants how they are expected to act and relate to each other towards achieving the purpose of the game. The rules reflect the values and culture of the game (e.g. competitive, collaborative, etc.) Through the common accepted rules, people feel a sense of membership and belonging in the community of participants.

- **Feedback**: Key Performance Indicators (value produced for customers, time to market, sustainable pace, number of defects, employee engagement, etc.) provide a sense of progress and accomplishment. With meaningful visible feedback, people can adjust their behavior in order to advance and experience a sense of mastery and happiness. Feedback also comes from Direct Experience and Leadership Storytelling as the participants write the story of the organization's Agile transformation.

- **Opt-in Participation**. Most people want to have some amount of control in their lives. When they choose to participate, they also feel a stronger sense of belonging. Control, belonging, and feedback lead to engagement and a strong sense of purpose and responsibility. Opt-in Participation is essential. It is an excellent way to avoid the disengagement that often results from coercive mandates.

How to Construct a Good Game

Apply Game Mechanics to meetings, tasks, projects, and initiatives to increase engagement, progress, and accountability. Strong games produce the best results. The key is to define the initiative in terms of the four components of a good game, and state the principles loudly and clearly. For example:

- The goals are ... so that ....

  - Our experiments with ... are complete. Now we need to decide what to do based on the results.

- The rules are ...

  - Be fully engaged in the discussion while you are in the room. If anyone needs to "check out" they may leave the room and return when they can be fully engaged.

- We will measure progress by .....

  - Posting the agenda items where everyone can see them and checking off each item as it is complete.

  - Taking a ten-minute break every hour.

- You are invited to participate.

  - Can we all agree to these goals, rules, and feedback?

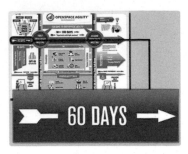

60 Days

It takes about 60 days to prepare for the first Open Space event and "100 Days" to Enterprise Agility. The organization is making a significant commitment by embarking on Agile transformation. True commitment to success begins with proper preparation and socialization throughout the organization.

The first two weeks (about 15 days) are for Leadership Preparation, Theme Crafting, and to Draft/Send an Invitation.

The next six weeks (about 45 days) are necessary for socializing OST-1.

These time recommendations are for a typical organization that plans to invite 200 or more people to the event. Smaller OpenSpace Agility implementations have been successful starting with less lead time. Proper preparation is critical. For this reason 60 days are recommended.

One dimension of the pre-work is creating and sending the Open Space Invitation. When a process-change is being introduced, it is essential for the affected people to have enough time to process "what it all means." Be sure to provide enough time for all invitees to examine the Invitation, consider it, discuss it with coworkers and friends, and decide whether to opt-in to living and writing the story of the organization's Agile transformation.

Theme Crafting

Each Open Space event must have a Theme. The Theme frames the experience. It serves as the high-level topic. It indicates the leadership team's vision, direction, and desire for creative input from the rest of the organization. A well-written Theme inspires the attendees to participate in writing the story.

The Theme is crafted in a facilitated meeting convened by the Sponsor. Ideally the Sponsor invites a sampling of people who represent a cross-section of the organization and they all show up.

The Theme is always framed as a question. For example:

- "How Can We Help Each Other?"
- "Why Agile Now?"
- "What must we do to beat our competition?"

The Theme must be wide enough to allow space for diverse topics and narrow enough to provide clear direction about the fundamental topic that needs to be addressed.

The wording of the Theme should also indicate these things in words or in tone:

- Some things are already known ("Why we need to act?").
- Some things are unknown ("How can we best act?").
- Some things are emerging ("What should we do?").

Draft/Send Invitation

People gather together in Open Space to discuss topics they are passionate about. The Sponsor is responsible for Drafting and Sending an Invitation for the event.

The Theme has already been developed and defined. The Theme Crafting meeting generated stories. If a cross-section of the organization participated, positive and supporting stories (signals) about the meeting have been spreading throughout the organization.

The Invitation provides a little more detail about the Theme, but not too much. The Invitation is an opt-in opportunity "to help write the story of the Agile adoption."

The Invitation must be written in a way that the story is not fully defined. The best kind of Invitation omits most of the details. Less is more. The goal is to inspire people to opt in and write the story.

The Invitation should:

- Demonstrate that the event is important to the Sponsor and to the organization.

- Provide just enough information about the Theme and the Open Space format so that people will be inspired to join.

- Indicate when the event will happen.

- Provide plenty of time for invitees to respond.

- Make it clear that participation is 100% optional.

Every Open Space event should be introduced by a genuine Invitation, meaning no one is forced to attend. There must be no real or imagined sanctions for anyone who declines.

It is best if the Sponsor writes the Invitation with some help from the Coach, who presumably knows and understands Open Space and OpenSpace Agility. The Coach can provide samples and encourage the Sponsor to write something similar in their own words.

In all cases the Sponsor should also send the Invitation. This signals that the event is important, and that responsibility for issuing the Invitation is not being "delegated down."

It is a good idea to leave plenty of time for responding. The invitees need to consider the Invitation carefully. Many of the people invited may be new to Open Space and may be hesitant at first. Allow sufficient time for the invitees to discuss the upcoming meeting, their ideas about the Theme, and whether they plan to attend.

In addition to the actual Invitation, it is important to create and distribute handbills and post them in public areas like kitchens, entrance doors, and hallways. The Sponsor may delegate the creation and posting of the handbills. The Invitation and the handbills confirm each other and make the event an obvious item to talk about in the days leading up to it.

45 Days

Theme Crafting is complete. The Sponsor has Drafted and Sent the Invitation to the First Open Space Meeting. Preparation continues during the next "45 Days."

- Distribute and post handbills throughout the building.

- Engage in Leadership Storytelling about Organizational Learning in the past and the potential for even more learning in the upcoming OST-1.

- Reinforce the fact that participation is 100% opt-in.

- Listen to the stories that members of the organization tell as they talk about the Invitation and what it really means.

The "45 Days" should be enough time for everyone to consider and process the Invitation to meet in Open Space. People need time to consider the Invitation and decide how to respond. This includes discussing the Invitation with friends and colleagues inside the organization.

The duration of 45 days is not a strict rule. In general, the more people you invite, the more time they will need.

First Open Space Meeting (OST-1)

The "60 Days" of preparation are complete. The Theme and Invitation have been developed, distributed, and socialized through the organization. The First Open Space Meeting has arrived!

OST-1 is the formal kickoff of OpenSpace Agility. It is a signal event.

Several things happen:

- The Participants learn how Open Space works.

- They experience diverse perspectives on the Agile adoption from diverse sources: Teams, executives, managers, directors, and Stakeholders.

- The Leadership team demonstrates their dedication to Open Space principles and to acting on the Proceedings.

For many Participants, Open Space will be a new experience. The experience of openness across the entire organization may be a novel experience as well.

During OST-1 the Participants identify and discuss important aspects of the Theme and how to experiment with Agile practices during the next "100 Days." They also learn that OST-2 has already been scheduled.

This authorizes everyone to suspend disbelief, act as if, and pretend that Agile practices might work while experimenting to identify the best practices. There is no need for mandates.

OPT-In Meeting: One Full Day

The First Open Space Meeting has two important characteristics:

- It must be completely opt-in, meaning it is 100% OK to opt-out, and OK to NOT attend.

- It is best for this event to last no longer than one day.

Open Space will be a new experience for many Participants. They might be unfamiliar with Agile values and principles.

It will take some time for the organization to integrate the learning and experience of the first Open Space event. A one-day event keeps it simple and allows the period of Experimentation to begin quickly.

The introduction of Agile affects people up, down, and across the entire organization. Inviting them to Open Space is one way to cross-pollinate these perspectives. The people invited might resist the idea of Agile. Or they may be merely tolerating the idea, with a "wait and see" attitude. Others may be strong supporters.

Attendance at the meeting must be opt-in. There cannot be any kind of pressure. Those who do not wish to attend must be afforded the opportunity to opt out without sanctions.

It is best for the event to include people from various positions and perspectives, people who are genuinely enthusiastic about exploring the Theme of the meeting as expressed in the Invitation.

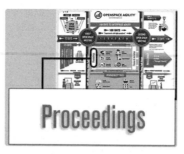

Proceedings from OST-1

Proceedings tell the story of the Open Space meeting and help the organization begin writing the story of the transformation.

These Proceedings serve to:

- Share each discussion with everyone in the organization.

- Document the important issues and recommended actions.

- Allow space for (Informal) Leaders to emerge. They identify themselves and take active roles in writing the story ("our story") of progress into Agility and high performance.

- Make it possible for the Sponsor to fulfill the commitment to act on the recommendations in the Proceedings.

Each Convener takes responsibility for inviting session Participants to contribute to the Proceedings so that they can share the outcome of their discussion with the entire organization.

- Proceedings contain handwritten or typed notes, diagrams, pictures, lists of session attendees, etc.

- They are collected by one or more Participants who agree to upload them immediately after the session.

- They are shared with the entire organization by a link via email no later than 24 hours after the end of OST-1.

Some Conveners become (Informal) Leaders in the process of improvement. Since OST-1 invites participation in the writing of the new story, the session Conveners tend to write the session reports without much help. They do benefit from some direction to ensure that the reports include recommendations as well as a list of attendees. The lists of attendees help identify emergent leaders as well as the people who might be willing to help around specific issues.

The Facilitator of OST-1 needs to support the Conveners and Participants to get the output from their sessions into the Proceedings as soon as possible during the event. This support will include sufficient input devices (e.g. laptops and cameras) at the event, space and tables for those input devices, and staff to support the effective use of those devices.

The timeliness of the publishing of Proceedings to all Participants is a critical element of Open Space. The Facilitator sets it up so that the Proceedings are complete very soon after the closing circle, ideally within a few hours. The distribution of the Proceedings should include a message from the Sponsor affirming that the organization will act on the top issues from the Proceedings as soon as possible.

The recommended approach is for the Sponsor to review the Proceedings and bring the most interested people together to identify, discuss, and act on:

- The most important concerns as reflected in the Proceedings.

- Recommendations from the Proceedings that can be implemented without additional authorization.

- The best recommendations that require additional authorization from the Sponsor, and how to get authorization.

- Recommendations that are beyond the Sponsor's authority.

CHAPTER 4

The Middle (Do)

Concepts

- Aligning with the Agile Manifesto values and principles
- Learning by experimenting with Agile practices
- Leadership and authority
- Storytelling

Context

- OST-1 revealed several areas that need to be addressed.

- The Sponsor acted quickly on the Proceedings and authorized Teams to select and begin experimenting with Agile practices.

- Leaders and Teams need coaching, encouragement, and reassurance as they experience new Agile ways of working.

- Nobody is really sure how the experiments will turn out.

Tasks

- Ensure that practices align with the Agile Manifesto.

- Conduct experiments long enough to understand whether the practice helps the Team do its work better.

- Allow the Teams to self-organize, so that leadership and authority emerge as Team members learn to lead and follow.

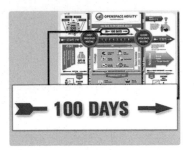

100 Days

One hundred days (16 weeks, 8 Iterations) is the recommended nominal period of time for Experimenting with Agile practices in OpenSpace Agility.

About 100 days gives the entire organization enough time to gain experience and to figure things out. Less time can work if it is carefully managed. As few as 60 days can be enough if the implementation is well-communicated and well-managed.

The "100 days" are bounded by OST-1 and OST-2.

During the "100 days," executives engage in Leadership Storytelling as they encourage Experiments with Agile practices. An "Agile practice" is any practice that supports (or does not offend) the four values and twelve principles of the Agile Manifesto.

Executives, directors, managers, and Teams are encouraged to suspend disbelief, act as if, and pretend that Agile practices can work as they experiment and learn.

The new learning is pulled into OST-2 where everything is inspected and everyone is encouraged to express what they want, think, and feel about the Agile adoption. In this manner, the free and open spirit of Open Space extends beyond the before-and- after meetings to include the entire period of learning.

Ideally, the OSA implementation creates fertile conditions for opening and holding "100 Days" of Open Space.

Time

Time creates boundaries that frame our experiences. Awareness that time is expiring can make it easier for people to suspend their disbelief, act as if, and pretend that new concepts can work. The same awareness can serve as a catalyst for getting things done.

OpenSpace Agility implements Agile in an Agile way, delivering incremental improvements frequently at a sustainable pace.

During the "100 days" between the two Open Space meetings, Experimentation and learning are encouraged. Predictable and reliable delivery of working software is the ultimate end goal. The journey starts with Experimentation, learning, and adaptation. All of this is bounded by time to produce a clearly-marked beginning, middle, and end for Participants.

The recommended amount of time between OST-1 and OST-2 is about 100 days. As few as 60 days can work provided all of the elements are carefully managed.

The key element to manage is communication about the next Open Space event. As the organization Experiments with Agile practices, it is essential to communicate continuously that the results of the experiments will be inspected carefully in OST-2.

In practical terms this means that everyone needs to know the exact date of OST-2. This also means that Formally Authorized Leaders (executives) need to communicate the date early and often.

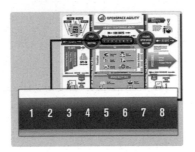

Iterations

The Agile Manifesto says to "deliver working software frequently" and that "at regular intervals, the team reflects and tunes and adjusts its behavior accordingly."

Iterative development is most appropriate when the work can be planned. This is not to say that Scrum must be used, or even that Iterations are required. The numbers 1 through 8 in the OpenSpace Agility Big Picture suggest Iterations, even though OSA does not strictly require that every Team must use them.

When the work cannot be planned, it may be more appropriate to use flow-based practices like Kanban.

Regardless of whether the practices focus on iterative development or on reducing work in process and cycle time, the Team should regularly reflect, tune, and adjust its behavior.

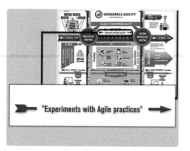

Experiments with Agile Practices

In OpenSpace Agility, Teams are authorized and encouraged to do Experiments with Agile practices and choose the most appropriate ones. It is best if they then tailor and tune these practices to fit their context.

The one constraint is the Agile Manifesto. Teams are taught the four values and twelve supporting principles of the Agile Manifesto, and then are encouraged to experiment with any practices that align with the Manifesto.

The two main outcomes of OSA are high employee engagement and continuous Organizational Learning.

Experiments with Agile practices engage people in direct learning experiences because they are:

- Authorized by executive leadership

- Celebrated through storytelling

- Confirmed by the Agile Manifesto

- Facilitated by process facilitators

- Time-boxed by the "100 Days" of Experimentation

- Conducted in the context of current projects

- Inspected and adjusted during the Second Open Space Meeting

Experiments Drive Learning

Organizational Learning happens when people question the way things are, try new things, and learn together.

Since there is no one specific way to "do" Agile but many ways to practice Agility, Experimentation explores what works and what doesn't for the people involved.

To avoid mandates or focusing on quickly finding the "right" way to implement Agile (which often results in rigid, sub-optimal practices), everybody is invited to experiment and create situations where learning can take place.

Leaders and initiators of new or established practices can emerge and become actors in the organization's now-emerging story of change and learning.

Some Agile practices are formalized and described in numerous sources including Scrum, Kanban, Extreme Programming, etc. Other Agile practices will emerge as things to try in accordance with the Agile Manifesto and the organization's purpose, culture, context, and situation. Questioning assumptions behind current practices by asking "Why are we doing this?" and articulating "We must assume x, y, and z" is a great way to explore answers to "What would Agile do?"

Fear and worry impede learning. When skepticism, worry, and resistance get in the way of Experimentation, it can be helpful to remind ourselves and others to:

- Suspend disbelief

- Act as if

- Pretend these practices can work

When experimenting, nothing is set in stone. All experiments will be subject to inspection and adjustment during the second Open Space where all voices are equally authorized and welcome to speak.

Agile Manifesto

In 2001, seventeen influential leaders of Extreme Programming, Scrum, Feature-Driven Development, and other agile practices met to discuss the fundamental values and principles of agile software development. Together they agreed upon and subsequently published the Agile Manifesto (www.agilemanifesto.org).

The Agile Manifesto is not perfect. However it is an essential yardstick and source of truth for organizations that are pursuing competency in Agile software development.

OpenSpace Agility practitioners agree that "Agile" practices are defined as those that align with the Agile Manifesto's four values and twelve supporting principles.

Traditional software development spends a lot of time and energy focused on processes and tools, producing comprehensive specification documents, negotiating detailed contracts, and strictly following plans. This approach makes it very difficult to adapt to changing business needs.

According to the Agile Manifesto, the more important values are individuals and interactions, working software, customer collaboration, and responding to change. Agile organizations should use processes and tools, appropriate documentation, contracts, and plans to support the more important values.

The twelve supporting principles describe how to create an Agile working environment.

Agile Values

We are uncovering better ways of developing
software by doing it and helping others do it.
Through this work we have come to value:

Individuals and interactions over processes and tools

Working software over comprehensive documentation

Customer collaboration over contract negotiation

Responding to change over following a plan

That is, while there is value in the items on
the right, we value the items on the left more.

Kent Beck	James Grenning	Robert C. Martin
Mike Beedle	Jim Highsmith	Steve Mellor
Arie van Bennekum	Andrew Hunt	Ken Schwaber
Alistair Cockburn	Ron Jeffries	Jeff Sutherland
Ward Cunningham	Jon Kern	Dave Thomas
Martin Fowler	Brian Marick	

Agile Principles

1. Our highest priority is to satisfy the customer through early and continuous delivery of valuable software.

2. Welcome changing requirements, even late in development. Agile processes harness change for the customer's competitive advantage.

3. Deliver working software frequently, from a couple of weeks to a couple of months, with a preference to the shorter timescale.

4. Business people and developers must work together daily throughout the project.

5. Build projects around motivated individuals. Give them the environment and support they need, and trust them to get the job done.

6. The most efficient and effective method of conveying information to and within a development team is face-to-face conversation.

7. Working software is the primary measure of progress.

8. Agile processes promote sustainable development. The sponsors, developers, and users should be able to maintain a constant pace indefinitely.

9. Continuous attention to technical excellence and good design enhances agility.

10. Simplicity–the art of maximizing the amount of work not done–is essential.

11. The best architectures, requirements, and designs emerge from self-organizing teams.

12. At regular intervals, the team reflects on how to become more effective, then tunes and adjusts its behavior accordingly.

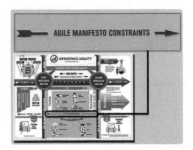

Agile Manifesto Constraints

The four values and twelve principles of the Agile Manifesto define the meaning of "Agile" in OpenSpace Agility.

There is one essential requirement or constraint when experimenting with Agile practices. All practices must support and align with the Agile Manifesto. At a minimum, each practice must not obviously offend the core values and supporting principles of the Manifesto.

It is a good idea to post the values and principles in team rooms and other places where everyone affected can be reminded of them. Everyone is encouraged to ask questions and insist that practices align with the Manifesto.

Minimal structure during the First Open Space and the Second Open Space encourages Participants to discuss a wide range of topics and ideas. As they experiment during the "100 Days," the Agile Manifesto provides just enough structure to make sure that they are really using Agile to experiment with Agile.

Do the current practices focus more on individuals and interactions than on processes and tools?

Do they support efforts to deliver working software without requiring comprehensive specifications and other documentation?

Do they encourage collaboration between customers and the Team instead of arguments about detailed contract specifications?

Do they support changing plans in response to changing needs?

If so, those practices are encouraged. If not, it is time to inspect more closely and change those practices.

Does the organization satisfy its customers by delivering valuable software or other products early, frequently, and continuously?

Do the processes harness change for the customer's competitive advantage?

Do business people and developers work together daily, preferably with face-to-face conversations?

Does the organization build projects around motivated Teams instead of trying to build Teams around valuable projects?

Is working software or other products the primary measure of progress?

Can sponsors and developers maintain a constant pace indefinitely?

Does the organization focus on technical excellence and good design?

Does it maximize the amount of work not done?

Do the Teams determine what work they take on, and how they do that work?

Does each Team regularly reflect and adjust its behavior to become more effective?

———

If the organization follows the four values and twelve principles of the Agile Manifesto, each of the answers will be "Yes!" Otherwise the practices must be changed.

The Agile Manifesto defines a clear boundary between agile (encouraged) practices and non-agile (discouraged) practices. Inside that boundary there is complete freedom for self-organization and Experimentation. The results can be amazing.

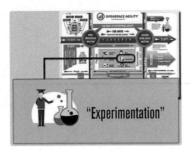

Experimentation

During the period between the First Open Space Meeting and the Second Open Space Meeting, Teams are encouraged to experiment within the guardrails of the agile principles.

With the number of failed Agile adoptions in the industry today, it is easy to understand how most people come to OpenSpace Agility with a certain amount of cynicism. OSA encourages Teams to suspend disbelief and experiment with various practices. When Teams see the specific practices they are using actually work, the cynicism slowly fades and the Team progresses in its journey to hyper productivity.

Experimentation is the key to creating the fertile conditions for continuous improvement across the organization.

To bring about change in an organization, the people need to change their behavior. People resist change and uncertainty.

Major transitions are fraught with stress and fear of the unknown.

As people learn the culture of the organization and how work gets done they become comfortable with the rules of the game. When a shift in how work is done is introduced, fear and uncertainty naturally follow. Experimentation can reduce this anxiety, since the changes must be proven to be successful. Without fear and anxiety about the changes, the experiments can be run for a specified length of time. Results of the experiments encourage new habits and changed behaviors.

Direct Experience

In OpenSpace Agility, factual reports and inspection of Direct Experience are valued over logical arguments, debates, and differences of opinion.

The reason is very simple: by the time we finish debating the relative merits of a given approach, we could have completed multiple experiments and received a valuable harvest of Direct Experience.

In other words, "Some things are better felt than tell't."

During the "100 days" between the two Open Space events, Participants are encouraged to conduct as many experiments as possible, consistent with the goal of continuous learning and continuous improvement for the enterprise as a whole.

Most of the people in OSA are problem-solvers. They become highly engaged around discovering and proving solutions to difficult problems. They value concrete evidence over exhaustive speculation about feelings, assumptions, and expected results.

Direct Experience is "unpacked" during periodic Open Space events. During these events, Participants are encouraged to express what they want, think, and feel about the use of Agile principles and related practices. They connect the dots and figure out the best ways to move the Agile transformation forward.

Emergent Leadership

Formally Authorized Leaders are assigned. (Informal) Leaders emerge.

- **Formally Authorized Leaders** take care of the organization's future results. They try to control engagement, progress, accountability, and authorization for people doing the work by using formal structures such as processes, tools, documentation, contracts, roles, and plans.

- **(Informal) Leaders** take care of people's need to belong in the organization. They influence engagement, progress, accountability, and authorization of the people in the organization by using informal or invisible structures such as norms, culture, stories, status, and relationships.

- **Emergent Leadership** is how the organization discovers hidden assets. Emergent leaders develop engagement, progress, accountability, and authorization within the organization by using fluid, temporary structures such as Invitation, Opt-In Participation, Direct Experience, stewardship, and personal development.

Organizational Learning and innovation reveal themselves via Emergent Leadership as a person takes initiative and leads something that they are passionate about and would like to try. When it's safe to suspend disbelief, act as if, and pretend that they can lead, the whole organization learns and discovers hidden value within its people and processes.

Formal and (Informal) Leaders have roles to play in encouraging Emergent Leadership:

- **Engagement**: For emergent leaders to step up and step outside of their comfort zones, they have to be invited to do so. Any perceived risk for stepping up will prevent people from trying, so there can be no formal assignment from Formal Leadership and no informal assignment or peer pressure from (Informal) Leaders. Invitation means anyone can accept and decline regardless of formal title and informal status.

- **Progress**: Progress during OpenSpace Agility is measured through stories about initiatives, experiments, emergent leaders, and direct learning experiences. Formally Authorized Leaders need to communicate and celebrate stories of safe space learning efforts regardless of the outcome. (Informal) Leaders need to support and encourage people to challenge their own learning edge.

- **Accountability**: Emergent leaders step up because they want to sharpen their alignment of purpose, autonomy, and mastery. They say: "I want to make this happen." Formally Authorized Leaders emphasize accountability through contracts and (Informal) Leaders emphasize relationships. Emergent leaders feel accountable to a personal purpose and to their Team's sense of autonomy and mastery (i.e. learning).

- **Authority**: Formally Authorized Leaders authorize work through making plans and (Informal) Leaders do so by responding to change. Emergent Leadership authorizes anyone to emerge as a leader and experiment within their temporary leadership role. Formally Authorized Leaders and (Informal) Leaders must allow and encourage Emergent Leadership. "May I lead this initiative?" is an Invitation that can be accepted or declined.

Leadership Storytelling

A large part of the culture of an organization is created and reflected by the stories told by its people. Stories about the past, the present, and the future help create a coherent narrative of who the organization is. The life of the organization is made alive through the telling and retelling of these stories.

When an organization and its people are going through change, the need for stories is elevated. People naturally look to their leaders to fill this gap. If the leaders fail to provide coherent narratives about change, then people will create stories themselves to make sense of the changes they experience. When stories are generated from reaction rather than intention, the stories may or may not support and align with the overall purpose of the change. When this happens, the organization risks creating a culture based on random, incoherent stories that do not align with organizational goals. This creates completely unnecessary and counterproductive levels of confusion, resistance, and fear.

Leaders can fill this void with purposeful storytelling and story generation. Successful organizational change happens when the purpose of change is communicated through coherent storytelling by Formally Authorized Leaders. Leadership Storytelling begins before the First Open Space Meeting and continues through the Experiments with Agile practices and OST-2, and carries on into the future as the organization continues to develop.

Past, Present, and Future

Telling positive stories about the past honors the people who participated in previous successes. It creates a coherent narrative by identifying strengths from the past that can create positive outcomes now. Since all change happens in the present, it is here that stories of Experimentation are shared: Who is trying what and what is the outcome? These stories speak to the nature of going through change by creating lots of learning experiments. Stories about the future are visions. These stories will inform how present activities will lead to future ways of working.

Story Generation

Telling stories about the past, present, and future helps create the coherent narrative of the flow of changes within the "100 Day" Rite of Passage. By engaging in deliberate, authentic actions and behaviors, leaders can generate stories about organizational change.

To generate stories, leaders must intentionally behave in ways consistent with the change story, and leave the storytelling to whoever will pick it up. Whatever the Formally Authorized Leaders pay attention to will signal importance to the rest of the organization.

People look to leaders to help make sense through change. Through Leadership Storytelling, change initiatives are more likely to actually take root and succeed.

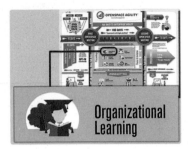

Organizational Learning

Organizational Learning is the key competitive advantage for modern day companies. The increasing complexity of technological advances makes it imperative to leverage the full combined brainpower of our Teams. When this is done, the result is collective success for the business.

Studies show that solutions derived from Teams are far better than solutions derived by individuals, even the "smartest" among them.

Learning and execution are often at odds; learning naturally brings us into the area of unknown and potential failures. In order to facilitate Organizational Learning, the culture has to permit Teams to fail fast and learn.

Organizational Learning drives innovation, which has a direct result on the bottom line of a corporation. In addition, if you read the tea leaves, you will see that the best talent in the up-and-coming workforce will only consider working in a learning organization.

Millennials are predicted to overtake the Boomers as the largest generation in the workforce in 2015. This generation has a very different mental model than all prior generations. They value an engaged workforce first and foremost. This is the networked culture, connected without constraint. They value collaboration and getting along over being right. Millennials love collaboration. In order to attract this up-and-coming talent pool, corporations need to create productive environments where teamwork thrives.

CHAPTER 5

The Ending (Check)

Concepts

- Preparing for the second Open Space

- New Theme and Invitation

- What should the organization do next?

Context

- The Teams have experienced Open Space so they know what to expect with OST-2 and self organization.

- The Teams have gained Direct Experience from experimenting with Agile practices for about 100 days. They have seen what worked and what did not, and they have learned how to align their practices with the Agile Manifesto.

- Time is running out. The Coach will depart soon. It is time for the Teams to level up and take responsibility for moving the Agile transformation forward.

- OST-2 serves as a passage rite as the current chapter of learning closes and a new chapter begins.

Tasks

- Craft the Theme for OST-2

- Draft and send the OST-2 Invitation

- Hold OST-2 and act on the Proceedings

Theme & Invitation

Theme & Invitation are critical components in planning and preparing the organization for each Open Space meeting. Before OST-1 they introduced Open Space, the Agile initiative, and the Theme, along with the importance of Opt-In Participation.

Toward the end of the "100 days" of Experiments with Agile practices, the organization will be expecting OST-2. And in general, the people who plan to attend will be well-prepared for it.

The story of the shifts that happened during the previous "100 days" will be fresh in their minds. They know about Proceedings and how quickly they will be distributed and acted upon. Leadership Storytelling during the previous "100 days" has been confirming and supporting the ongoing process of Experimentation.

There is also an emergent awareness of the most difficult obstacles facing the organization and the goal of continuous improvement. People are aware of the upcoming Coaching Role Change and the reduced availability of the Coach.

Time is running out.

In helping the Sponsor craft the Theme & Invitation for OST-2, the Coaches can change tactics and speak more directly. Their roles will change soon. They must "sharpen their rhetoric."

OST-2 will be less novel and will tend to have lower attendance. Those who do participate will be better prepared and ready to tackle clearly identified issues with greater focus and commitment.

Second Open Space Meeting (OST-2)

The Second Open Space Meeting will be different than OST-1.

- Everyone knows how Open Space works. The original novelty of Open Space is no longer present.

- It is not just a prospective meeting that looks forward, but it is also a retrospective that looks back.

- Everyone has observed and experienced how Formally Authorized Leaders behaved after OST-1 and during the "100 Days."

- Some of the resisters may have become tolerators or even supporters of Agile principles.

- Tolerators may now support Agile transformation.

- Everyone has a very good idea of where everyone else stands with respect to the process of experimenting with Agile principles and practices.

- The easy-to-remove impediments are mostly dealt with, and some very thorny problems and issues remain.

- Those who are prone to "gaming the system" are likely to be conspiring about how to "play" and participate in the OST-2 event.

The Sponsor can harness this energy by focusing on removing obstacles described in the Proceedings. So here is what you can expect:

- Lower attendance overall. OST-1 attendance included some curiosity seekers. They tend not to attend OST-2.

- The topics tend to be much more focused on a few big issues, the major things that are holding back the next level of progress.

- The closing circle is smaller.

- The Coach is leaving or otherwise shifting to a substantially new role, for example: Shifting from coaching Teams to coaching just product owners, Facilitators, Scrum Masters, or executives.

The OST-2 event is an important inspection point. During this meeting the organization inspects the outcomes of the last "100 days" of Experiments with Agile practices.

Practices that are not clearly working are adjusted, tailored, or even discarded as a result of discussions inside this meeting.

Impediments to continuous improvement tend to be clearly identified and discussed.

OST-2 is a call to action.

The OST-2 meeting also has a high concentration of people who are truly committed to continuous improvement. The people who attend OST-2 are the people who like the very open approach and the very strong results of OpenSpace Agility.

OPT-IN Meeting Two Full Days

The Second Open Space Meeting is a great place to define and execute actions. The group has experienced OST-1 and "100 Days" of Experiments with Agile practices. The group as a whole knows the issues, the opportunities, and the problems.

Individual members of the organization have a very good idea about who is currently supporting the process of change – and who is not.

For these reasons, OST-2 can be a longer meeting. A two-day event allows time for identifying issues, solving problems, and taking action. The participants can move to action immediately in a way that extends beyond Formally Authorized Leaders and includes everyone present. OST-2 is about sharpening focus, intentions, and results. It is about taking action.

An excellent way to sequence OST-2 is to start it on the afternoon of the first day, and continue for a full second day. This wider period of time can include activities at the end that create Energy, Action, and "Escape Velocity" on the issues that are most important to address and solve.

During the last part of the second day, the Facilitator can include activities to encourage ownership of and action on the issues that are holding the group back. The "100 days" are over and people are feeling empowered. OST-2 is a great place for Formally Authorized Leaders to signal that the group has enough authorization ("permission") to take up the leadership of the Agile adoption and achieve Escape Velocity for themselves.

www.OpenSpaceAgility.com

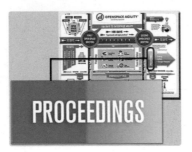

Proceedings from OST-2

The Proceedings for the Second Open Space Meeting serve many of the same functions of the Proceedings of OST-1 and require most of the same support.

But there are significant differences:

- People understand the process and require less direction and hand-holding.

- OST-2 usually has a smaller but more determined attendance. Those who do attend typically show up with a much higher level of commitment and focus.

- The topic list is shorter and tends to focus on the biggest obstacles and impediments in the way of a high performing and learning organization.

- A similar post-OST inspection meeting happens, but the role of the Coach changes or even ends after the leadership inspects the OST-2 Proceedings. The Coaches sharpen their rhetoric in anticipation of the change in their role. The Proceedings of OST-2 are a rich source of material for the sharpened rhetoric. With these Proceedings the Coach can underline critical items for the leadership to heed.

After OST-2, the focused and committed Emergent Leadership will tend to experience the Coach-role change as a signal to "step it up." They now understand what needs to happen to "level up."

CHAPTER 6

Ongoing (Act)

Concepts

- One chapter ends, another begins

- Reflect, inspect, and adjust behavior

- Recurring Open Space

Context

- This chapter of Organizational Learning is complete. Issues emerged in OST-1. Leaders acted on those issues and authorized Teams to conduct experiments during a specific window of time.

- The most engaged people attended OST-2 and identified the remaining big issues. Leaders acted on Proceedings and authorized the Teams to proceed.

- The people have experienced self organization, control, and they have a sense of progress as they graduated to a new level.

Tasks

- Change the role of the Coaches

- Schedule the next recurring Open Space

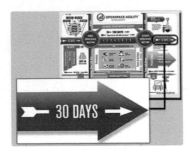

30 Days

The Second Open Space Meeting is a closure event. It establishes the boundary between the previous chapter of Organizational Learning and the next one. It is the final point in the organizational passage rite. For the passage rite to be most effective, the organization must have a sense of "leveling up" or graduating.

The Coach should vacate the organization for at least 30 days following OST-2. Doing so promotes a strong sense of progress and moving to the next level. It supports feelings of graduation.

If the coaching role does not change, there is a diminished sense of progress. The role must change. The goal of OpenSpace Agility is to bring the organization to a state of self-sustaining, freestanding agility as soon as possible. For this to happen, the Coach's role and perceived authority within the Teams must diminish.

The "30 day" period following OST-2 is a time for the people to integrate their learning from OST-1, Experimentation, and OST-2. It is a time to reflect on what they have learned, to inspect the results, and to tune and adjust their behavior.

This is a good time to ask some questions including:

- Have champions for the Agile transformation emerged?

- Can you identify them by name?

- How rapidly has the organization acted on the Proceedings from OST-1 and OST-2?

- What kinds of actions is the organization taking without being directly prompted by the Coach?

- What is happening in terms of people, plans, and policies as a result of OpenSpace Agility?

- Is the organization making substantial changes?

- What are the results of the initial 100-day experiments with Agile practices?

- Have the Teams learned to tailor their practices to align with the Agile Manifesto in order that they might do their work better?

Coaching Role Changes

One of the fundamental concepts of OpenSpace Agility is that people feel good when they experience a sense of progress.

In gaming, "leveling up" delivers a sense of progress. In standard implementations of Agile, the same coaches might stay with the same Teams for years. This becomes an impediment for Teams who are looking for a sense of progress and specific events that demonstrate progress.

Coaches must continuously reaffirm that their role is entirely temporary in nature. The Coaches must communicate to the executives, directors, managers, and Teams that they must begin the challenging (and rewarding) process of learning how to reach a state of freestanding and self-sustaining Agility for themselves. This means being able to continuously improve, without the need for an external authority called "Coach" telling them what they "should" do.

Organizations make progress in small steps and will need some amount of coaching along the way. The organization needs to feel a sense of progress as they close the previous chapter of Organizational Learning and begin a new one. The Coach was an authority figure in the previous chapter. When the Coach vacates that role and moves on to work with other Teams or in other organizations, the previous Teams level up and begin writing the next chapter of their Agile transformation story.

Coaching may continue in the new chapter, but with a different Coach and a different Master of Ceremonies.

The entire purpose of shifting the role of the Coach is to deliver a sense of "leveling up" and progress as the entire organization moves along its transformation journey. Periods of Organizational Learning are framed by Open Space events that serve to punctuate the end of one chapter and the beginning of another.

The Open Space events are important rituals or ceremonies that define boundaries by time and experience. This is the progression of ceremony and ritual that we know from our school years. As we progress through the grades, graduation ceremonies punctuate the end of one learning experience and the start of a new one.

And so it is the same with OSA.

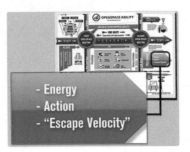

Energy, Action, Escape Velocity

By the time the Second Open Space Meeting rolls around, people are energized and ready to take action. They have experimented with Agile practices in an open environment. During OST-2 they look back and they look forward to the next step in escaping from the practices that did not work.

Encourage and initiate action inside OST-2 rather than waiting for Formally Authorized Leaders to act in a certain way. This is the time and place to encourage even higher levels of engagement and commitment. Wise Formally Authorized Leaders can direct that energy as they signal the areas in which the group is empowered to take action.

OST-2 is typically characterized by three or four big issues that stand in the way and need to be resolved. There may be a need for product road-mapping at the enterprise level. Or there may be existing policies or roles that need to be amended or completely abolished because they stand as impediments to continuous improvement. There will be problems that are big, need attention, and require action.

To address these issues and maintain forward momentum, it is best to encourage problem-solving action inside OST-2. The Coach, Open Space Facilitator, and Sponsor should work together to architect some activities inside this meeting that will strongly encourage action on and ownership of problem-solving.

It is imperative that all of this is duly authorized by the Sponsor.

Ideally, this is the state of being for the organization after OST-2:

- The group can clearly identify the top issues of immediate concern.

- Each issue has a champion who brings passion and responsibility to the task of addressing and solving the problem.

- Each issue has a wider team who pitches in to help.

- For each issue, the champion and the Team have very clear agreement about who is doing what to address the issue after OST-2. In this manner a sense of progress across the entire organization begins to manifest. Before long, the culture starts to tip in the direction of continuous improvement and a strong intention to create great results.

When this happens, many impediments tend to go away, as those who are not really supporting the new culture realize that more than a few things have changed in the past "100 days." The culture is actually shifting and approaching the escape velocity it needs in order to continue moving forward.

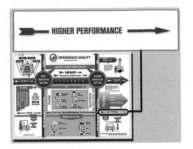

Higher Performance

Organizations use OpenSpace Agility with intent to create Higher Performance. Higher Performance emerges team by team as the transformation journey progresses.

Enough structure is provided to allow Teams to learn and experiment with various Agile practices. The ultimate goal is to find a set of Agile practices that accelerates performance.

Once team members experience the power of autonomous decision-making regarding how they work, they begin to sharpen their ability and motivation to sense areas in need of attention. This increased engagement leads to even higher performance.

When a team hits its stride, the positivity is infectious. After awhile the entire culture starts to value continuous improvement. When this happens the culture is truly shifting.

Recurring Open Space

In practical terms, the organization is now thinking much more independently and is much more responsible for its own learning. In symbolic terms, a change in coach status is essential and is emphasized throughout the passage rite process to underscore the fact that the organization is making progress integrating Agile ideas into the cultural fabric of the organization.

The last aspect of OpenSpace Agility is the biannual Open Space meeting. Held in January and July, these events are important and essential. The whole organization anticipates them. They also serve as a place for initiating new hires into the culture.

By including these recurring cultural events on the organization's calendar, the risk of dependency on any one leader is greatly reduced and might even be eliminated. A typical failure pattern in the adoption of Agile occurs when a highly authorized Sponsor and progressive leader exits the company. The safe space necessary to do Agile well departs with that leader.

Instituting recurring semiannual Open Space events provides a framework for continuing the Agile transformation regardless of whether previous Sponsors are still with the organization.

CHAPTER 7

OpenSpace Agility Theory

OpenSpace Agility is built on some core ideas from the psychology of games and cultural anthropology. These are described in some detail below. It is important to understand the theory of OSA before implementing it, so be sure to examine this chapter carefully.

Happiness

Work can be viewed as a game. If the core requirements for happiness at work are not present, people disengage and check out. If the core requirements are there, they automatically experience fun, satisfaction, and potentially a deeply engaged sense of well-being. OpenSpace Agility delivers happiness through the intentional design and implementation of good-Game Mechanics.

Work is BROKEN when it is not fun to play. Deliver happiness at work by injecting good-Game Mechanics into the structure of work and meetings.

The core requirements for happiness at work are:

- A sense of control

- A sense of progress

- A sense of belonging and membership

- A sense of wider purpose and meaning

When viewed in this way, it is possible to more fully design the interactions, meetings, and work itself so that participating is optimized toward a satisfying, fun, and naturally productive experience.

OpenSpace Agility employs Game Mechanics to make Agile adoption enjoyable and fun.

Games

Games have four basic properties. When the values for each of the properties are "well-formed," the game is enjoyable, fun, and satisfying. When the four properties are not "well-formed," the game is not fun and people either opt-out or, if this is not possible, they disengage ("check out") almost automatically.

The 4 basic properties of a good game are:

- A clear goal

- A clear set of rules that are uniformly applied

- A clear way to get feedback and to track progress

- Opt-In Participation

Well-executed Agile patterns and practices are usually (but not always) well-formed games. Well-formed games associate with satisfaction, happiness, and even joyfulness; poorly defined games associate with disengagement, low levels of learning, and a distinct lack of enjoyment.

OpenSpace Agility makes culture change easier by making it a good game. The key gaming component is the Invitation, which is used instead of a mandate. Participants are invited to experiment with Agile practices, instead of being forced to use them without being part of the decision-making process.

Culture is a game, and Agile culture is no exception. Agile adoptions are games. To make Agile adoptions fun, we must tune up four properties: the goals, rules, feedback loops, and ability to opt in or out of playing the game. In OpenSpace Agility, a focus on Game Mechanics is essential.

Invitation, Opt-In, and Engagement

Mandates reduce engagement, and they have the potential to ruin your Agile adoption. The mandate of Agile practices reduces the potential for genuine engagement.

Invitation increases engagement by offering options. A sense of control and a feeling of belonging are sources of basic human happiness. Opting in or out of an Invitation increases the sense of control. Accepting an Invitation increases the sense of belonging and inclusion.

Mandating Agile practices seldom works because there is no opt-in feature to the game. This makes it less than fun to play because the game is not "well-formed." This may seem counter-Intuitive. However, mandates reduce engagement, the fuel of rapid and lasting Agile adoptions. Invitation is a far better approach. It aligns with the Agile Manifesto's core principles.

Consider these quotes from Martin Fowler, a signatory of the Agile Manifesto:

> *"A team may choose a totally waterfall, un-agile process. In that case, clearly the process is no more agile than apples taste of strawberries. But agile methods aren't the best for all situations, and personally I'd rather have a team work in a non-agile manner they chose themselves than have my favorite agile practices imposed upon them."*
> *–Martin Fowler, "AgileImposition" blog post, 2006*

Here are more quotes from that same essay:

> *"Imposing an agile process from the outside strips the team of the self-determination which is at the heart of agile thinking."*

> *"... imposing agile methods introduces a conflict with the values and principles that underlie agile methods."*

> *"So I hope I've made clear that imposing agile methods is a very red flag."*

OpenSpace Agility is a good game, partly because of its opt-in nature. Invitation can engage the independent thinkers in your organization. They are the ones who can help create success with Agile.

Liminality and Learning

The liminal state is a transitional state of being. The root Latin word – limens – means "threshold." The liminal state is a no-man's land of transition, confusion, stress, and vagueness. It lacks definition. No longer where you were, and not yet where you will end up, liminality has the potential to drive people crazy.

Liminality is a stressful state of being that occurs in transitions. Agile transformation requires adopting new ways of thinking. This change can cause considerable worry and anxiety. As a solution, OpenSpace Agility uses a well-understood cultural device called the "passage rite" to manage liminality and reduce stress.

Adopting Agile always means lots and lots of new learning. Learning is stressful, because it means going through transition. All genuine learning in adults creates instability and stress until that learning is integrated.

On Mental Models

We know the world through our models. Mature adults hold a model of reality, and genuine new learning challenges the validity of that model. This invalidation of previous assumptions produces an unstable state until the new understanding is integrated.

The introduction of Agile into an organization definitely creates liminality. The introduction of Agile is usually a trigger for most participants. This "triggered" behavior is based on fear and is a natural reaction to entering the unstable state of liminality.

Before Agile, roles and methods of interaction were well understood. New roles and new ways of interacting require a new mind-set. The process of learning can be very stressful.

When faced with an uncomfortable transition, the natural and safe thing to do is turn around and go back. People in organizations routinely do exactly this. They backslide on Agile and return to where they came from. This "going back" reduces worry, fear, and anxiety, the core emotions evoked by the liminal state of being.

Rites of Passage

Passage rites have been used for thousands of years to manage stressful transitions in human experience. OpenSpace Agility implements a passage rite that begins and ends with an Open Space meeting event. This brings structure to the chaos associated with integrating new learning.

Various tribal societies throughout the world and across different time periods have reached the exact same conclusion: Liminality must be handled carefully. The best way to handle it is with a passage rite.

The purpose of a passage rite is to ease the transition from one state of being to another. Tribal societies have been practicing passage rites for thousands of years.

In the modern day, we routinely introduce Agile into organizations, while blissfully ignoring the essential human dynamics of liminality.

This is a serious error, one that OSA is keen to avoid.

Stability in the Liminal State

A hypothesis of OpenSpace Agility is that introducing Agile into typical organizations creates liminality at the group level. If this liminality is handled with a passage rite, there is potential for a rapid and lasting Agile adoption.

The core idea behind OpenSpace Agility is that recognizing and addressing liminality reduces the worry, anxiety, and fear associated with Agile adoption. It creates at least the potential for a rapid and lasting Agile adoption. The primary way this is accomplished is by leveraging the ancient practice of the passage rite. A passage rite creates a structured experience for participants with a beginning, middle, and end.

OpenSpace Agility is a repeatable technique for getting a rapid and lasting Agile adoption. It works with what you are currently doing and can be added at any time. It incorporates passage rites, Game Mechanics, Open Space, storytelling, and more, so your Agile adoption can take root.

The Passage Rite

Transitions are difficult. Adopting Agile is a big transition that always means lots and lots of new learning and the stress of liminality. The primary way to manage this kind of stress in a social system is to institute a passage rite, a ritual whose structure defines the beginning, middle, and end of a transitional experience.

Experience Design

Designing a passage rite is an exercise in experience design. Passage rites serve as containers that reduce the highly destabilizing feelings of liminality. This is important, because the stress can lead to all sorts of problems, including deep anxiety, fear, panic, depression, and even various forms of neuroses.

Passage rites usually include at least one very scary experience. For example: A member of a tribe in Africa going through a passage rite from boyhood to manhood might have to kill a dangerous animal like a lion or a hyena. You might be wondering if this passage-rite notion is such a good idea. Do we really want to put people though super-scary experiences?

Here is something to think about. Culturally speaking, what comes first: the highly stressful transition, or the passage rite?

Passage Rites and Liminality

The highly stressful transition comes first. Passage rites are a cultural response. They serve to contain the scary experience of transition. They are established by a culture in response to the need to manage highly stressful liminality. The transition comes first; the passage rite comes later as a cultural mechanism for managing the transition from here to there.

In other words, a passage rite does not produce stress. Instead, a passage rite manages the liminality that arises during key transitions in the life of the group and its members.

The stressful and necessary transition – for example, the transition from childhood to adulthood – is present BEFORE a passage rite was instituted.

The primary task of an Agile adoption is to produce a cultural transformation. This is a huge transition that in theory never ends because it is focused on continuous learning and improvement.

Managing huge transitions is difficult. Passage rites help people make the transition to a new state.

Passage Rites as Culture Games

Passage rites are cultural games. They are designed with a clear goal, clear rules, rich feedback, and Opt-In Participation.

- Big transitions in the life of a group produce liminality.

- Liminality is stressful. It can make you anxious and fearful.

- Passage rites are cultural devices that help handle the liminal state of being, so that the participants can get through to where they need to go.

- Agile adoptions are transitions. They produce considerable anxiety, worry, and the liminal state.

- A formal passage rite – a certain kind of cultural ritual – can help participants close one chapter and open a new one.

- OpenSpace Agility works because it acknowledges these dynamics and institutes a rite of passage that helps all the participants in an Agile adoption get from where they are to where they need to go.

- Passage rites are designed games that emerge from necessity in a culture to help it thrive.

Play and Experimentation

Let's just tell it like it is: Agile is a learning framework that is based on frequent experimentation. All experimentation is play, and Agile learning is playful. OpenSpace Agility supports and strongly encourages experimentation and genuine playfulness. OSA frames Agile experience as a series of experiments. What is really going on is play, and play is fun.

Communitas

Agile adoptions thrive on strong feelings of communitas. It is "the spirit of community." When the spirit of community is "up," the space is open, and the feeling of communitas is strong. When the spirit of community is "down," the space is closed, and the communitas is weak.

Example: If you love going to work, the overall spirit at work is probably "up." If you cannot wait till Friday, the overall spirit in that workplace is probably "down."

With respect to Agile adoptions, communitas is essential. It comes from clearly understood and uniformly applied rules. It comes from a sense that everyone is engaged. It comes from a sense that we are all going through this together.

During Agile adoptions, everyone is being triggered. What is my role? What are the rules? When does this end? What does this mean for my status in the group? Executive leaders are triggered. Managers are triggered. Team members are triggered. A new game with new rules is stressful. In a no-man's land of new rules, new roles, and unfamiliar ways of working, is it any wonder Agile adoptions routinely fail?

Passage rites can help generate communitas – the very spirit of community. Cultural anthropology says that people going through a passage rite do in fact have the same status during the passage. Participants have widely varied status, going in.

Then the communitas kicks in – all are coming from a known place, and going to an unknown place. All of them make the difficult and even dangerous passage together. And after it is over, all have changed from what they were to what they now are. Passage rites can help ease the liminality of transition.

Passage rites are intentionally designed cultural experiences. Repeat: Passage rites are intentionally designed cultural experiences. They are cultural-experience designs. Passage rites are designed to create feelings of community.

Agile adoptions generate a steady stream of stressful liminality, because the learning in Agile is constant. "Continuous improvement" is the goal. That generates a ton of stress on the culture. Learning is change, and change is stressful because it produces liminality. The passage rite is a cultural device for handling liminality.

Passage rites bring communitas, and communitas brings at least some (and maybe more than a little) comfort. All of the participants going through the passage rite experience a beginning, a middle, and an end. They experience it together, regardless of level of authorization. Everyone is learning.

This structuring of the unstructured is very comforting, and reduces worries – and stress. Passage rites are extremely useful devices for helping you obtain a rapid and lasting Agile adoption.

OpenSpace Agility is a repeatable technique for getting a rapid and lasting Agile adoption. It works with what you are currently doing, and can be added at any time. It incorporates the power of Invitation, Open Space, passage rites, Game Mechanics, storytelling, and more, so your Agile adoption can take root.

Open Space: Passion and Responsibility

The Open Space meeting format is designed to generate very high levels of engagement. It does so by getting all the people with a sense of passion and responsibility in one place, at one time, to address matters of importance to all Participants. OpenSpace Agility uses Open Space to generate Invitation and engagement.

The Master of Ceremonies

Every legitimate rite of passage is a designed cultural experience, and OpenSpace Agility is no exception. Part of the design is the "Master of Ceremonies" role.

The Master of Ceremonies is an essential role in the passage rite event. The Master of Ceremonies helps to maintain the structure and makes sure that the passage rite is executed well. The Master of Ceremonies is a kind of referee that works in service to everyone experiencing the liminal state of transition. In OpenSpace Agility, the person in the Coach role functions as the Master of Ceremonies during the passage rite.

It is important to note here that the Sponsor cannot act as the Master of Ceremonies. This is because the Sponsor is actually a Participant with everyone else in the passage rite.

Storytelling

"...the name of the game is Collective Storytelling. This process may begin with the leader's tale."
—Harrison Owen, The SPIRIT Book, p. 112

In OpenSpace Agility, deliberate storytelling is essential. Storytelling is well understood to be essential to the generation of culture. In OSA, leaders engage in deliberate acts of narrative creation with a specific focus on telling stories using past, present, and future tense.

Semiotics & Signaling

We navigate the world via signs and signals. In organizations, the leaders' behavior is the primary signal. Leaders provide signals about where we are and where we are going. We look for these signs and signals, and use them to navigate. Inside OpenSpace Agility, leaders integrate the idea of signaling into everything they do. People tell stories about leader behavior. In OSA, leaders are "tuned in" to storytelling.

Stories are signals and signs in a culture.

The Sense of Progress: The Coach Role Changes over Time

In OpenSpace Agility, a segment of learning bounded by two Open Space events is called a Chapter. Each Chapter represents a passage, and progress. In OSA, the role of the Coach changes formally at the end of each Chapter. This creates a sense of graduating and "leveling up."

Announcing the fact that the Coach role is going to change as of the next Open Space meeting is an essential aspect of OSA. This announcement signals that the Teams and everyone else involved need to get busy assuming more and more responsibility for moving the Agile adoption forward.

It is essential that the role of the Coach diminish with each Chapter that starts and ends in Open Space. This reduction in the authority of the Coach has a symbolic and practical aspect. In practical terms, the Teams must know that the Coach cannot be depended upon to answer all questions forever, and that they must mature to the point where they need little (if any) coaching to continuously improve. In symbolic terms, the reduction of the authority of the Coach means that the Teams are assuming at least some (if not all) of the authority the Coach originally started with.

With each Open Space event, the authority of the Coach is decreasing formally. This is important for delivering a periodic and strong sense of progress across the entire organization. Without this change in the status of the Coach, there is no progress and in fact no passage from here to there.

The entire job of the Coach is to get the organization to a place where the employees are taking total responsibility for their own learning. This does not happen all at once.

Recurring Cultural Ritual

OpenSpace Agility implements a series of passage rites designed to enable a rapid and lasting Agile adoption. Each passage ritual begins and ends with an Open Space meeting. These rituals enable the group to reduce the stress associated with the transition to Agile.

What happens after that? In OpenSpace Agility, this pattern of the periodic passage rite becomes part of the culture. Genuine Agile creates at least the potential for continuous learning. With continuous learning comes continuous liminality. A key feature of OSA is the institution of periodic and recurring Open Space meetings, typically in January and July each year. These meetings are cultural ceremonies – rituals. These meetings serve as milestones and important cultural checkpoints. The fixed scheduling of these events forms a container for the learning and the liminality that comes with it. These cultural events support the continuous learning that an Agile culture creates. These cultural events in January and June also serve to initiate new hires into the organization's culture of learning.

Glossary

OpenSpace Agility derives from Prime/OS, a more general framework for process-change in organizations.

Prime/OS is open-source culture technology that anyone can use to create derivative works. You can learn more about Prime/OS at: www.Prime-OS.com

Listed below are the OpenSpace Agility™ and Prime/OS™ terms of art:

Authority: The right to do work. See also **BART**.

Authority Projection: The almost automatic characterization of the Prime/OS™ consultant as an authority figure, often leading to various impediments to progress within the client organization.

BART: An acronym representing Boundary, Authority, Role, and Task.

Chapter of Learning: In Prime/OS, the period bounded by a beginning and ending Open Space event. In Prime/OS, a Chapter lasts at least 90 days.

Consent: Willing, opt-in support for a proposal.

Communitas: The spirit of community, as described in the works of Victor Turner and others. See also **Turner, Victor**.

Culture Game, The: A book by Daniel Mezick that asserts that culture is experienced as a game by all the members. See also **Mezick, Daniel**.

Denning, Steven: Author of the book *Leadership Storytelling* (see also), which is a useful tool for examination by Formally Authorized Leaders considering using the Prime/OS™ methodology.

Facilitator: In Open Space and other meeting formats, a role occupied by a person who works to make the process easier for members to participate in and enjoy.

Game Mechanics: The specific features of a game that define how effective the game is in creating engagement. Well-formed games have well-formed Game Mechanics, especially the following features: clear goal(s), clear rules, a clear way to track progress, and opt-in participation.

GPL: The "General Purpose License," an open-source license for software and written works which encourages innovation and collaborative development.

Group Relations: A community of practice focused on the study of leadership, authority, and unconscious processes in groups.

Invitation: In Prime/OS™, the offered opportunity, by formally authorized organizational leaders, to act or engage in an activity. Typically this means attending an organizational event or participate in a process. Genuine Invitations do not have sanctions or any other implied or expressed (negative) consequences.

Liminality: An unstable state of transition between two states. A person is said to be experiencing liminality when engaged to be married, changing jobs, or moving residence from one place to another. An organization is said to be liminal when it is moving from one way of working to another, for example during the initial stages of adopting new methodologies, organizing structures, or learning new processes. See also **Turner, Victor**.

Leadership Storytelling: In Prime/OS™, the act of filling a social space with meaning in order to reduce anxieties, worries, and liminality in the organization. Also the title of a useful book by Steven Denning. See also **Liminality**.

Mandate: In a process of organizational change, a command or other communication that creates compulsory participation without regard for what the participant wants, thinks, or feels. See also **Invitation**.

Master of Ceremonies: In a passage rite, an essential role. In Prime/OS™, this role is occupied by the Prime/OS™ practitioner, typically an organizational consultant.

McGonigal, Jane: Author of *Reality is Broken*.

Mezick, Daniel: Author of *The Culture Game* and originator of the Prime/OS™ methodology. See also **Culture Game, The**.

Open Source: A type of license that promotes attribution, innovation, community, and collaborative effort. Prime/OS™ is published as open source culture technology. See also **GPL**.

Open Space: A meeting format with related planning, arranging, execution, and after-event follow-up. The Open Space meeting format supports and encourages self-organization and self-management. See also **Open Space Technology, A User's Guide**.

Open Space Technology, A User's Guide: A book by Harrison Owen describing the Open Space meeting format.

Opt-in Participation: A truly voluntary choice to participate in response to an Invitation. In a game, a feature of "good-game" mechanics. All good games have clear goals, clear rules, a way to track progress, and opt-in participation. See also **Mandate**.

Owen, Harrison: Originator and formulator (with others) of Open Space, a meeting format with related processes that support and encourage high levels of group-level self-management and self-organization.

Passage Rite: In cultural anthropology, a ritual in which the social status of the participants changes. The Prime/OS™ methodology facilitates the design and construction of a passage rite for modern teams, tribes, and business enterprises. See also **Liminality**, **Communitas**, **Master of Ceremonies**.

Quiet Period: In Prime/OS™, a period of 30 days following a passage-rite period of at least 90 days. The passage rite in Prime/OS™ starts and ends with an Open Space event of at least one day. During the Quiet Period, the Prime/OS™ consultant does not communicate with the organization.

Reality is Broken: An important book by Jane McGonigal. This book provides a useful and clear definition for the word "game"; see page 22. See also **McGonigal, Jane**.

Signal Event: In Prime/OS, an action by Formally Authorized Leaders that indicates a shift in company culture in the direction of more openness, enterprise-wide dialogue, and innovation across the organization.

Signaling: The transmission of communication from a sender to a receiver. Signaling can be either verbal or non-verbal, or a combination of both. Signaling is an important topic of study for leaders who are considering Prime/OS as a method of igniting engagement throughout the enterprise.

Turner, Victor: Author of several important books in the domain of cultural anthropology that have influenced the formulation of Prime/OS and derivative works that are built upon it, such as OpenSpace Agility.

Selected Bibliography

Note: By far the most important book in this list is *SPIRIT: Development and Transformation in Organizations*, by Harrison Owen. You can obtain it for free here: http://www.openspaceworld.com/Spirit.pdf

Bion, W. R. (1961). Experiences in Groups: and Other Papers. London, UK: Tavistock Publications. [Print].

Booth, S. L., & Meadows, D. L. (2010). The Systems Thinking Playbook: Exercises to Stretch and Build Learning and Systems Thinking Capabilities. White River Junction, VT: Chelsea Green Publications. [Print].

Cockburn, A. (2007). Agile Software Development: The Cooperative Game. (2nd ed.). Upper Saddle River, NJ: Addison-Wesley. [Print].

Csikszentmihalyi, M. (1990). Flow: The Psychology of Optimal Experience. New York, NY, USA: Harper & Row. [Print].

Denning, S. The Leader's Guide to Storytelling: Mastering the Art and Discipline of Business Narrative. USA: Jossey Bass. [Print].

Gharajedaghi, J. (2006). Systems Thinking: Managing Chaos and Complexity: a Plat-form for Designing Business Architecture. (2nd ed.). Amsterdam, NL: Elsevier. [Print].

Fowler, M. (October 2, 2006). AgileImposition. www.martinfowler.com/bliki/AgileImposition.html

Godin, S. (2008). Tribes: We need you to lead us. New York: Portfolio. [Print].

Hsieh, T. (2010). Delivering Happiness: a Path to Profits, Passion, and Purpose. New York: Business Plus. [Print].

Kline, P., & Saunders, B. (1998). Ten Steps to a Learning Organization. (2nd ed.). Arlington, VA: Great Ocean. [Print].

Logan, D., King, J. P., & Fischer-Wright, H. (2008). Tribal Leadership: Leveraging Natural Groups to Build a Thriving Organization. New York: Collins. [Print].

Margolis, M. (2009). Believe Me: Why Your Vision, Brand, and Leadership Need a Bigger Story. New York: Get Storied. [Print].

May, Matthew E. (2009). In Pursuit of Elegance: Why the Best Ideas Have Something Missing. New York: Broadway. [Print].

May, M. E. (2011). The Shibumi Strategy: a Powerful Way to Create Meaningful Change. San Francisco, CA: Jossey-Bass. [Print].

McGonigal, J. (2011). Reality Is Broken: Why Games Make Us Better and How They Can Change the World. New York: Penguin. [Print].

Mezick, D. (2012) The Culture Game: Tool for the Agile Manager. USA. Freestanding Press. [Print].

Owen, H. (2008). Open Space Technology: a User's Guide. (3rd ed.). San Francisco, CA: Berrett-Koehler. [Print].

Owen, H. (1987). Spirit: Transformation and Development in Organizations. Potomac, MD: Abbott Publishing. [Print]. http://www.openspaceworld.com/Spirit.pdf

Owen, H. (2000). The Power of Spirit: How Organizations Transform. San Francisco: Berrett-Koehler. [Print].

Owen, H. (1999). The Spirit of Leadership: Liberating the Leader in Each of Us. San Francisco, CA: Berrett-Koehler. [Print].

Owen, H. (2008). Wave Rider: Leadership for High Performance in a Self-organizing World. San Francisco: Berrett-Koehler. [Print].

Senge, P. M. (1990). The Fifth Discipline: the Art and Practice of the Learning Organization. New York: Doubleday/Currency. [Print].

Sinek, S. (2009). Start with Why: How Great Leaders Inspire Everyone to Take Action. New York: Penguin Group. [Print].

Thomas, D., & Brown, J. S. (2011). A New Culture of Learning: Cultivating the Imagination for a World of Constant Change. Lexington, KY: CreateSpace. [Print].

Turner, V., (2001) From Ritual to Theatre: The Human Seriousness of Play, PAJ Publications. [Print].

About the Authors
OSA Certified Trainer: Daniel Mezick

Daniel Mezick is an author, executive and Agile coach, and keynote speaker. He is the formulator of OpenSpace Agility.

He is the author of *The Culture Game*, a book describing 16 patterns of group behavior that help make any team smarter. The book is based on five years of experience coaching 119 Agile teams across 25 different organizations.

Daniel's client list includes CapitalOne, INTUIT, The Hartford, Cigna, SIEMENS Healthcare, Harvard University, and many smaller enterprises.

Daniel is based in Guilford, Connecticut.

Web: www.DanielMezick.com

Email: dan@newtechusa.net

OSA Certified Trainer: Deborah Pontes

Deborah Pontes is the agile transformation leader at the QuickBase division of INTUIT. She leads lasting organizational change through team empowerment and increased transparency.

Her passion is to drive alignment of purpose and shared understanding of current state. She strives to make readily available, easily digestible information the backbone of the organizational culture.

Deb's entire career has been in software delivery. The past six years have been in service to better agile teams through facilitation of non-mandated agile practices at CIDC, PerkinElmer and INTUIT.

Deborah is based in Boston, Massachusetts.

Web: www.openspaceagility.com/consulting/

Email: dpontes09@gmail.com

OSA Certified Trainer: Harold Shinsato

Harold Shinsato is an Agile coach-developer and culture hacker. As Executive Director of Montana Agile Culture House, he has helped facilitate culture change in Western Montana through the use of Open Space Technology and other unconference derivatives of OST.

Harold has helped bring culture change through Open Space to SAP, Intuit, Capital One, MIT's Medicine Hackathons, the University of Montana, and more.

Harold is an Associate Certified Coach with the International Coaching Federation. He has years of Open Space facilitation experience and sits on board of the Open Space Institute.

Harold has over a decade of Agile experience that includes bringing eXtreme Programming to software teams, and serving as a Scrum Master. He has given presentations at Agile conferences including Agile 2011, Agile CultureCon, and AgileOpen events, and has multiple trainings from Agile Learning Labs & the Agile Coaching Institute.

Harold has been trained and mentored directly by the originator of OpenSpace Agility, Daniel Mezick, and has collaborated with him on many projects.

Harold is based in Missoula, Montana.

Web: www.shinsato.com

Email: harold@shinsato.com

OSA Certified Trainer: Louise Kold-Taylor

Louise Kold-Taylor works with a network of partners helping individuals, teams, and organizations through Agile transformations using approaches from coaching, team facilitation, community organizing, and organization development.

Louise holds a M.Sc. in Engineering as well as certifications as Life Coach, Team Coach, ScrumMaster, Agile Facilitator, and OpenSpace Agility Trainer. She is currently pursuing a Master's degree in Human Systems Intervention at Concordia University. Before becoming a coach, Louise worked eight years in biomedical research and urban planning.

With a sense of care and respect for the people she coaches, a session with Louise often feels like a quality encounter with a good friend. Her specialty is helping people dealing with complexity and developing perspectives that bring ease, enjoyment, and common sense to their team's collaboration and organizational culture.

Louise is based in Montreal, Canada, as well as Copenhagen, Denmark.

Web: www.lentascoaching.com

Email: louise@lentascoaching.com

OSA Certified Trainer: Mark Sheffield

Mark Sheffield is an Agile coach, IT consultant, and Open Space Technology facilitator. Mark increases engagement in agile adoptions by focusing on creating environments with clear goals, clear rules, visible feedback, and opt-in participation. Instead of concentrating on a particular framework, he invites teams to experiment with Agile practices while abiding by the values and principles of the Agile Manifesto.

Mark has over five years of Agile experience in addition to holding ScrumMaster and Product Owner certifications from Scrum Alliance, Inc. He has over 20 years of IT experience including software development, firewall management, and Electronic Data Interchange.

Mark is based in High Point, North Carolina.

Web: www.marksheffield.com

Email: mark@marksheffield.com

Notes

Notes

Notes

Notes

Notes

Made in the USA
San Bernardino, CA
18 October 2018